COWGIRLS
early images and collectibles

Judy Crandall

**With
Price Guide**

77 Lower Valley Road, Atglen, PA 19310

DEDICATION

This study of the American Cowgirl is dedicated to the two most important men in my life;

To my dad, Bob Neulreich who brought me West when a mere child and taught me that through faith and hard work, nothing is impossible.

To my loving husband, Jerry Crandall who introduced me to the treasure that is the historic Old West and who provides me with security to pursue my dreams.

Copyright © 1994 by Judy Crandall
Library of Congress Catalog Number: 94-66778

Printed in The United States of America
ISBN: 0-88740-646-7

We are interested in hearing from authors
with book ideas on related topics

Published by Schiffer Publishing Ltd.
77 Lower Valley Road
Atglen, PA 19310
Please write for a free catalog.
This book may be purchased from the publisher.
Please include $2.95 postage.
Try your bookstore first.

One of the more desirable photographic collectibles is this incredible view taken by Marcell during the Pendleton Round Up in 1911, the first year cowgirls officially participated in this rodeo. Depicting all the ladies on horseback, this image measures an incredible 48 inches long and 8 inches tall. In the author's collection, it is believed to be one of two in existence. *Author's collection*

"Cow Girls" at the PENDLETON

CONTENTS

Christmas, 1994

To my sweet-sweet Angie,
                                   You are the apple
of my eye. Every day you bring me joy
+ happiness. I love to watch you play
with your brothers and sisters. You are
growing up into a lovely little lady, and
I am so proud of you. You are such a smart
little girl !! I'll love you always little sweetheart,
                                                   Love Dad
                                                   xxxx

"Up" 1911

Official Photos
Copyright 1911 by
Marcell
of Portland

ACKNOWLEDGEMENTS

Preparation of a book such as this requires an enormous amount of research and organization. Many people helped in my endeavor to produce the first book dedicated to the American cowgirl and the collectibles she provided.

By including my personal collection, and adding collections of some fellow enthusiasts, I believe assembled here is one of the most comprehensive, all around books on the subject. We have not only reproduced, in one publication, the most important selections of postcard and photographic images but also show some of the three dimensional collectibles available.

My deepest, heartfelt thanks are extended to the numerous friends both old and new who answered my pleas for help during the creation of this book. Thanks to Tona Blake who sent me a tape of period music which I listened to while writing this book; to LaVaughn Bresnahan, historian and photo research librarian from Wyoming State Museum; to Jim Burk, noted stuntman who paved the path to Polly Burson's door where I found a first hand account of what the rodeo cowgirl experienced. Thanks to Bob Butterfield, John Kopec, Linda Rose, Tom Martin, and Lang Spraggins, fellow collectors who always let me know about available cowgirl items. To Jack Davis owner of Old America Antiques, Montana's only antique post card and paper shop who generously gave of his time and collection so that this book may be complete.

Thanks to Dottie Galloway for reading the manuscript and making constructive suggestions. Thank you, too Mary Lou Hammer wife of rodeo promoter Candy Hammer, who gave me some first hand information which was invaluable. Thanks to Jim Marck at Marwest Photo Service who met my unrealistic photographic requirements and to Jeff Millet who, many years ago said, "Judy, why don't you do a book on cowgirls?", well Jeff, I have! To James Nottage, Chief Curator at the Gene Autry Western Heritage Museum for meeting my impossible deadline. A special thanks to the ladies from the National Cowgirl Hall of Fame and Western Heritage Center, Virginia and Margaret who assisted with much of the research.

Thank you to Stephanie Qualls, curator at the National Cowboy Hall of Fame for finding those lovely saddle photos. And, thanks to Phil and Linda Spangenberger who so generously helped with the three dimensional collectibles section; a special thanks to Kim and Dave Viers whose enthusiasm for my project spurred me on. And speaking of spurs, I couldn't have done this without Frank Costanza, of Costanza's Custom Saddles in Stevensville, Montana, who was always ready with an encouraging word when I needed it.

Over the 20 years that I have been interested in and collecting the various items from the era of the American Cowgirl, there have been many people who touched my life. Fellow collectors are a terrific group of people and my warmest thanks to each and everyone who I have encountered in my collecting.

Judy Crandall
Sedona, Arizona 1994

It is unfortunate that the identities of these cowgirls as well as the location of this delightful image is unknown.

Note their split riding skirts made of either leather or corduroy, probably dating it to pre 1925. Also recognize how the cowgirl on the far left keeps the burro from upsetting the scene - she not only holds his ear but is making him forget the uncomfortable position he is in by curling his lip inside out!

This Doubleday postcard is entitled "Bronc Riders and Good Ones." *Wyoming State Museum*

INTRODUCTION

In the field of western memorabilia, the rodeo cowgirls provide the collector with items of rarity as perhaps no other area does. From around 1900 through 1940 women competed in the rodeos alongside men for cash prizes as well as for exhibition money and in so doing unknowingly created a distinct area of western collectibles. At times these pioneering competitors were regarded as something of a spectacle, watched because they were different. Yet the early cowgirl, by participating in this purely American sport, was perhaps our first professional woman athlete.

During those formative years women were allowed to compete by performing the same rodeo events as the men. They rode broncs, even though many hobbled their stirrups under the horse's belly, rode bulls, bulldogged, (wrestled steers) and roped. They also rode Roman style races, relay races, flat races and performed death defying tricks on horseback. Many were proficient with rope tricks as well. During these days the competitors were called 'contest hands' as opposed to the term 'arena cowboy' used today.

Women who competed during these early years generally came from the Wild West shows, ranching and circus backgrounds. Many times, the girls would try their hand at rodeo, then go back and forth between circus performances and rodeo events in an effort to earn as much money as possible. With the end of the Wild West show era many cowgirls and cowboys needed to find work and the rodeo arena seemed to be a natural for them.

However, in 1929, during the well publicized Pendleton Round Up held annually in Oregon, a popular cowgirl Bonnie McCarroll died as a direct result of injuries received during a bucking horse contest. She was not the only female fatality this sport experienced yet this incident coupled with the apparent decline of the rodeo, possibly due to the depression, contributed to the end of the so-called dangerous competitions for the rodeo cowgirl. Rather than endanger the lives of the women riders, many rodeo promoters and arena directors contracted with the cowgirls for exhibition riding, paying them a flat fee rather than have them compete for cash prizes. In spite of these changes, the relay race competition which, for all intents and purposes, began participation in rodeo for women, remained the most popular event with both the cowgirls and the fans until its termination in 1946.

Many times these early cowgirls would be referred to as 'World Champion' and there seemed to be quite a few of them. The reason apparently stems from the fact that official rodeo event records were not kept until 1929 at which time the World Champions were declared by point scores won at Rodeo Association of America member rodeos. Across the United States, before 1929, the title World Champion was awarded to each event winner according to the particular rules for that rodeo, and the performers continued to use the title throughout the balance of their careers. Those titles bestowed upon a competitor prior to 1929 were in truth useless in the eyes of the Rodeo Association of America. Nevertheless, many cowboys and cowgirls kept their World Champion title.

Rodeo contestants would advertise their availability in publications such as The Billboard. Arena directors and promoters would contact these rodeo people and invite them to participate in their rodeos. In this manner, the cowgirls and cowboys would set up their 11 month, January to November schedule called rodeoing, which is called a circuit today. Many times a name performer had many more offers than he or she could accept, a fact which the promoter could count on to draw larger crowds. Participants would travel from city to city often camping along the way as hotels were scarce and horse boarding even more so!

Even though the turn of the century Wild West shows played overseas, the true rodeo was not introduced to European audiences until 1924 when Tex Austin took his troupe to England's Wembley Stadium. This exhibition was so well received that even after Austin left, a small group stayed overseas to travel major European cities to the delight of all who were fortunate to attend their shows. Several more rodeo shows were organized for the European audience yet none received the rave reviews and attendance like that of the first one.

Finding collectibles from the early rodeo cowgirl of the Golden West is more difficult than one would think. For every 20 or so cowboys there was 1 cowgirl, so the number of items left is small. The most readily available item is the photo postcard image of the cowgirl. Items such as saddles, spurs, cuffs and bridles have been absorbed into the Wild West collectibles for there is little or no difference between cowboy and cowgirl use of these items with perhaps the exception of the saddles used by the trick riders, or maybe smaller spurs for little feet. Skirts, vests, hats, gloves, scarves and the like are around but are very rare with most examples in various museum collections.

The image of the cowgirl has been romantically captured by artists of the period. From advertising to fantasy images of what the "Cow Girl of the West" was, can be found in art cards which are rare but available.

What the reader will find in these pages is not only the collectibility of the cowgirl items from postcards to split skirts but also the history of these remarkable women. In photo collecting, the history of that person in the image is rarely known. Rodeo cowgirls for the most part, were celebrities of their time. This book tells their fascinating history from voices of the past spoken through photos and artifacts from the Cowgirls of the Golden West.

POSTCARD IMAGES OF THE RODEO COWGIRL

Postcard images of all kinds have been popular since before the turn of the century with just about everyone using the 'penny postcard' to communicate with family and friends. Currently, postcard collecting is one of the top five hobbies in the world and is increasing in popularity every year.

With the universal fascination of the Wild West, it was a natural progression for the rodeo performers, cowboys and cowgirls to be a featured topic on these cards. The photo postcard has evolved as a window to history which includes the photographer who took the image, the ladies' appearance, and what the rodeo itself must have been like.

During the early rodeo days there were several photographers who specialized in chronicling this unique western sport. Most famous of these was Ralph R. Doubleday who, for nearly 40 years carried his camera into the leading rodeos across the country. It is believed that he took the first picture of an airborne cowboy flying off a bronc. This cowboy was Gus Nylen who 'dismounted' at the Cheyenne Rodeo in 1910.

Will Rogers, a true rodeo fan, stated in one of his editorials that "...Doubleday had made at least ninety-percent of all the good rodeo pictures ever made...". "Dub" Doubleday, through his thrilling images, promoted widespread fascination for rodeo more so than perhaps any other individual. "I always rode the horse with the cowboy," Dub stated, "and just when I felt I was going to buck off, I snapped the shutter."

Not only are his images packed full of action, they were also readily accessible, as Dub was very prolific which increased his popularity. Additionally, he was a terrific promoter possessing an innate sense for merchandising. Oftentimes he would have images taken during the rodeo available for sale to the public the very next day. While it is impossible to accurately count total sales, it is believed that Dub parlayed his 20,000 images into over 30 million copies sold.

Doubleday marketed his images to periodicals, made postcards, worked with dude ranch guests, and created a deck of playing cards. Dub had worked out a rodeo card deck which included producers, top hands, cowgirls, clowns and the like. His initial print run was 50,000 with the second order just six months later for another 50,000. The question the collector raises is, where are these card decks?

Using a seemingly clumsy, but not for him, 5X7 plate portrait Graflex camera, Dub created the sharpest pictures in the business. Another Graflex user was John Stryker who worked out of Fort Worth Texas. Stryker's hallmark was his angle of view. By holding his camera almost at ground level he created a ground blur in the foreground. Almost all of his images have this out-of-focus patch which aids in creating an almost larger than life impression of the rodeo performer. Unlike the prolific Doubleday, Stryker created only about 3,000 images.

Another important figure in the rodeo arena was DeVere Helfrich from Klamath Falls, Oregon, who often tackled the impossible by shooting at night and indoors, a feat which neither Doubleday nor Stryker would attempt. Throughout his career which began in 1941 he took over 18,000 images.

Foster Photo Company operated by Foster himself was located in Miles City, Montana. Even though Foster contracted much of his work to Doubleday, he also published postcards of several Montana Rodeos including the Miles City Round Up and the Bozeman Round Up, both recognized as the two largest Montana rodeos of their times. W.S. Bowman worked in Oregon for a time with the Pendleton Round Up, who along with many others, took photos and later made them into postcards which have evolved into highly sought after collectibles.

One of the more obscure photographers was Will Stecker whose only touch with rodeo was in Gilman, Montana. Only a very few of these images have survived the test of time and they are included in this collection. Stecker hailed from Missouri, was educated at the Eastman School of Photography and traveled west in 1907. Upon arrival in Great Falls, Montana legend has it that he encountered the great western artist Charlie Russell who eventually encouraged the man to settle there. Will Stecker was moderately successful in selling his pictures in Montana; however, he maintained that sales went down when the postage went up to three cents a card.

Typically the names of the cowgirls and/or the location of the rodeo were written directly on the face of the image making identification of the girls more easily accomplished. Through first person accounts, various articles both of the period and as recent as 10 to 20 years ago about rodeo, a few books, and museum research, the biographies of these personalities can be constructed. Often, a cowgirl's name is buried in articles about her famous cowboy husband for many of the ladies married but few had children. Not every rodeo cowgirl who performed from 1900 to 1940 is represented here but rather these biographies simply augment the beautiful postcard images.

As the careers of these amazing women unfold, it quickly becomes obvious that it was an exciting time for the cowgirl. We are thankful we are able to enrich our lives with her memory through the necessary items of her day which have evolved for us as cowgirl collectibles.

CHAPTER 1

THE INDIVIDUAL COWGIRLS

Not all the early performing cowgirls are represented here. Rather this is a collection of photo postcard images which are reinforced by the ladies' individual stories. Some were photographed more than others, some are not identified yet included for the sake of history and still other images are here due to their rarity.

Selecting which images to include was not predicated on the quality necessarily of that image but rather on its historical significance. Therefore, some may appear to be of lesser grade which is not a direct result of printing but rather of the photo postcard itself. Some of these cards enjoyed a past of being stored in a box whereas many of them managed somehow to survive the ravages of the US Mail. They are, after all, postcards and the collector is fortunate to have access to what images are currently available.

Action scenes and studio posed images are second to the group photos in the eyes of the collector. The Doubleday and Stryker cards were produced in greater quantities than most other photographers' images making them more plentiful yet still somewhat hard to find. Photos taken at smaller rodeos such as Kissimmee, Florida, the Los Angeles Rodeo, Tucumcari and even the 1924 Tex Austin tour in England are also scarce. Several private rodeos throughout the west were rarely photographed; however, some were and those images are practically priceless. Even though images taken at Cheyenne Frontier Days and Pendleton are more readily available than those from the smaller rodeos, all cowgirl postcards are becoming more and more collectible due to their scarcity.

Strong personalities coupled with terrific images of these cowgirls emerge after experiencing this collection of rare photo postcards featuring the rodeo cowgirl of the Golden West.

TILLIE BALDWIN

In a rare action scene is Tillie Baldwin riding in the relay event. Note the cowboy's legs just behind her horse.

Tillie was a very colorful character who was known to "toss a mean rope." After immigrating to the United States from Norway, she worked for a very short time on Staten Island as a hairdresser. During her rodeo career she wore her long, golden locks neatly braided which can be seen in this image as reaching to about her waist. *Wyoming State Museum*

Trick riding in a long skirt could have been termed dangerous, nevertheless here is Tillie Baldwin at the Pendleton Round Up doing just that as photographed by O.G. Allen in 1912.

Tillie's birth name was Mathilda Winger. Not feeling this name had a terrific ring to it, she changed it to Tillie Baldwin after joining up with Captain Jack Baldwin's Wild West Show. It is believed that she simply liked the name but had no relationship with Captain Jack. *Author's Collection*

ROMAN RACE, RIDERS, JOHNNIE MULLENS, TILLIE BALDWIN & A.J. BRYSON, WINNIPEG "STAMPEDE" 1913.

Tillie Baldwin is shown in this rare Winnipeg Canada postcard winning the Roman Race in 1913. She is competing with the men named Johnnie Mullens and A.J. Bryson. This is a very rare image as not only is it from Canada, but it indicates the unusual situation of the women competing with the men in the same contest. *Author's collection*

W.S. Bowman captured Tillie Baldwin at the Round Up in Pendleton in this rare postcard of her coming out from "going under" the horse's belly.

Like her contemporaries she was a talented performer for in addition to her rope tricks she also competed at the 1916 New York Stampede, listed with Bea Kirnan, Lottie Vondreau and Peggy Warren. *From the private collection of Jack Davis, Olde America Antiques*

W.S. BOWMAN PHOTO NO. 246. TILLIE BALDWIN IN FANCY RIDING. ROUND UP LET'ER BUCK.

BERTHA KAEPERNIK BLANCETT

This W.S. Bowman photo shows Bertha Blancett, Champion Lady Bronco Buster of the World at the Pendleton Oregon Round Up.

In 1975 Bertha Kaepernik Blancett became one of the first cowgirl honorees inducted into the Cowboy Hall of Fame in Oklahoma City. In fact she was a charter member. Born on September 4, 1883 she lived to the age of 95.

Widely recognized as the first female bronc rider at the Cheyenne Frontier Days in 1904, Bertha Kaepernik brought a roaring crowd to their feet as she successfully rode a C.B. Irwin bucking roan horse. The year after her now famous ride, she rode her horse from Sterling Colorado leading a borrowed bucking horse to Cheyenne in order to compete. She is known as rodeo history's first cowgirl bronc rider.

Bertha joined the Pawnee Bill's Historic Wild West Show in 1906; she later joined Miller Brothers 101 Ranch Show where she met her future husband, Del Blancett a famous bulldogger. They were married in 1909 during the Detroit Show. With many other rodeo performers the Blancetts traveled to Australia with the Atkinson Show in 1912. After this show folded, they stayed an additional nine months down under working on a Queensland ranch. Over the course of their marriage, they had no children.

At the Pendleton Round Up in 1911, the first year women officially competed at Pendleton, Bertha easily won the woman's bucking horse championship, riding slick. When a cowgirl 'rode slick' this means she did not have the stirrups hobbled under the horses belly. Bertha would return many times to Pendleton winning bucking horse championships again in 1912 and in 1914. It was in 1914 that she came within 12 points of winning the all-around Championship of the Round Up. As far as the cowboys were concerned this was too close a tally, so the rules were changed separating women into their own category. Winning the relay race in 1911, 1912 and 1913 she was awarded the Silver Cup after having won the race two years in a row. In addition, Bertha Blancett rode in the 1914 Calgary Stampede Rodeo.

Many rodeo performers were willing players for the Hollywood Producers and Bertha was no exception. During an exhibition in 1913 of the 101 Ranch Wild West Show with whom she was riding at the time, Bison Pictures used the show as a backdrop for their feature picture COWBOY SPORTS AND PASTIMES which starred Bertha Blancett and a new actor Ed "Hoot" Gibson. A few other movies appealed to her but the call of the rodeo arena was overwhelming to the young performer.

At a rodeo in Walla Walla, Washington in 1915, Bertha Blancett won handily over the men contestants in the Roman style race, setting and holding the half mile track record yet to be broken. Bertha weighed in a healthy 165 pounds which she said contributed to her ability to ride Roman. She would shift her weight from horse to horse allowing for faster going on the track!

Because she had married a bulldogger, Del taught his wife to work for him as a hazer, a feat at which she became quite successful. Del's promising career was cut short during WWI when he joined a Canadian cavalry outfit serving overseas with famed Lord Strathmore Horse Unit. While in France, he was killed in the service of his country. Bertha never remarried.

Even though 1918 was her last year of competition at Pendleton, over the next few years she continued her connection with rodeo working as a pick-up rider. In 1921 she returned as a guest of the Round Up committee wearing a gold star on her sleeve in memory of her husband.

Her later years were filled with horseback activities as she ran a successful pack string and guide service in Yosemite National Park from 1922 to 1930. Bertha Blancett retired from rodeo in 1934, returning in 1961 to serve as Grand Marshall in the Pendleton Round Up Parade.

She was inducted into the Rodeo Hall of Fame in 1975. Bertha Blancett passed away in Porterville, California in 1979. *Author's Collection*

FAYE JOHNSON BLESING

Doing the classic Hippodrome stand is Faye Johnson Blesing in this postcard image from the mid 1930s. Faye was a headliner with the Madison Square Garden Championship Rodeo for seven years. Due to her popularity and beauty she was often asked to do commercial endorsements for saddles, western clothing, cigarettes and war bonds. The Stetson hat company even featured "the Faye Blesing Crease." *Wyoming State Museum*

In this Forth Worth Stryker Photo Faye Blessing performs a true crowd pleasing fancy or trick riding exhibition. A rare linen postcard, on the reverse is printed "Genuine 'Reinbeau' brand post card, made only for John A. Stryker, Western Photographer, Fort Worth, Texas."

Upon marrying Wag Blesing, noted cowboy who rode bareback, saddlebroncs, bulls and bull dogging, they became known as the Sweethearts of the Rodeo.

After a successful career in rodeo, Faye turned to the movie industry doubling as stunt woman for most of the noted actresses of the day. She has been honored by the National Cowgirl Hall of Fame. *From the private collection of Jack Davis, Olde America Antiques*

One of the rare DeVere photo postcards, here is Pee Wee Burge, a
leading bronc rider in the 40s. She rides *Upper Deck* during the
Escalon, California rodeo in 1946. *Author's Collection*

POLLY BURSON

Polly Burson began rodeoing at the young
age of 10 following in the footsteps of her
mother. Here is Polly winning the Denver
Post Trophy during the Cheyenne Frontier
Days Rodeo in 1939. According to Polly.

"...Frankie Burns owned the
horses. I would start on the horse
on the right. Boy he was a knothead,
crazy but he could run. Getting off
him running as fast as he could was
quite a little chore! That's my husband holding the middle horse. You
know, I never lost a horse, I'd get a
hold of the horn and got flying on
with the first jerk out of the station
putting me on that horse. That third
horse was a mare, she would save
herself 'cause I knew she had more
run left in her. When she would turn
to come on in home she would be
doggin' it on the back side then she
would speed up and come into the
station...it would part your hair! "
Courtesy Polly Burson

Polly Burson studied with Vera McGinnis, actually living with the famous cowgirl for six months. During this time she met Bonnie Gray, Dorothy Morrell and others who taught her some fancy riding horse tricks. Here Polly performs for a crowd doing some 'ground work',

"...where you hit the ground to a split to the neck or a reverse crupper from behind the horse or somersault off the side of the horse, you hit the ground and go back. Anytime you hit the ground it's called ground work. Top work is only tricks on the horse, not touching the ground, like drags and stands and so forth."

During Polly's era, 1938 to 1945, trick riding was a contract event, not a contest yet Polly did do a contest trick riding event early in her career at the Salinas Rodeo. "You win it by the tricks that you do, the ease with which you do them and the showmanship. You're judged on your ability to carry out the trick and sell it to the public." *Courtesy Polly Burson*

Polly is seen in this rare photo performing the Hippodrome which is how many of the performers would enter the arena. They would all stand on their horse, gallop around the arena while waving to the crowd as they were introduced, ending up in a corner of the arena from which they would individually perform their stunts.

Here is Polly on her favorite trick horse *Pierre.*

"..I bought that horse from Lucyle Richards in the lights of a car at night. I really loved that horse, he was more like a brother to me, you know. He made a living for me as I trick rode on him but I had him put to sleep when he was 31 years old!" *Courtesy Polly Burson*

Polly Burson traveled to Europe in 1956 with a group of rodeo performers one of whom was Faye Blesing, Polly's best friend. In this rare arena photo is a view of cowgirls and cowboys performing the Quadrille or Dance of the Ranch on horseback in Marseille, France. Polly is in the center. This performance was a contract act with everyone expected to be available to ride in the quadrille when they signed their rodeo contract.

Done to the strains of square dance type music, this was done purely for crowd entertainment. Taking up the entire arena, the riders rode very fast in the patterns.

"..I have a bad knee from a horse falling with me in Phoenix one year when I was just 15, and everytime I ever hurt anything in the quadrille, it was that damn knee. You know, those cowboys would get a little too wild and they would make you take out..when they turn, you gotta turn. The money we made from the quadrille was our drinking money as we called it. It was great fun!" *Courtesy Polly Burson*

KITTY CANUTT

Not many photos exist of Kitty Canutt; however, three of the better action bronc scenes are of the petite cowgirl. Here she rides *Eucalyptus* in this Doubleday postcard taken during a Lewiston, Idaho rodeo.

Kitty Canutt was the wife of Yakima Canutt, famous rodeo cowboy who during the heyday of the "B" western movies became a famed stuntman and actor. Kitty had a few small parts in the movies, however she never did any stunt or other injurious work. It is well known that Kitty had diamonds set in her front teeth which she often pawned when times were financially tough. *National Cowgirl Hall of Fame*

In a very rare Winnemucca Rodeo photo taken by Meyers this 1919 postcard shows Kitty Canutt high in the sky on a bronc. It appears she is riding with her stirrups hobbled, tied together under the belly of the horse. Cowboys in the early days believed that the cowgirls stood a better chance of staying on the bronc if the stirrups were hobbled. This proved to be a very dangerous practice as several women were seriously injured, even killed by using hobbled stirrups. *From the private collection of Jack Davis, Olde America Antiques*

A Doubleday postcard of Kitty Canutt on *Hell Diver* during the Spencer Iowa Round Up, R.G. Bangs, Manager. A terrific bronc pose shows this remarkable lady well-balanced in a wild ride. *Author's Collection*

MISS CANADA KID

A grand bucking photo by O'Neil Photo Company shows Mrs. Canda (Canada) Kid on a wild one during Iowa's Championship Rodeo held in Sidney, Iowa. Another rare image of a small rodeo yet an identified participant. *From the private collection of Jack Davis, Olde America Antiques*

GENE KRIEG CREED

During the Los Angeles Round Up Gene Krieg was captured by Doubleday on the bronc *Silvertip*.

Born in Missouri the family eventually settled in Holly, Colorado where she performed her first event standing on a galloping horse down the main street of her new home town. At the early age of 15 Gene participated in her first rodeo during the Watermelon Day Parade in Rocky Ford, Colorado. The next year, in 1925 she was crowned Queen of the Arena as World Champion Cowgirl during the Frontier Days in Cheyenne, Wyoming. During the Cheyenne Frontier Days, this title was bestowed upon one talented cowgirl who rode the best bronc. Along with the title she received the World Title, a trophy, $500, and immense popularity.

Things happened fast in this talented lady's career as the Frontier Days producer from Pendleton Round Up offered her expenses and $500 to participate in the Chicago relay races. In spite of the fact that she had only a few days to learn this event, she nevertheless accepted the challenge.

Over the years she was admired by the public and press alike for her amazing horsemanship and beauty. Over two years she carried on a relationship with cowboy Loyce *Shorty* Creed as they met on the rodeo circuit performing in the same round ups. They married in 1931 following a rodeo in Borger, Texas and honeymooned at a round up in Belle Fourche, South Dakota.

Gene oftentimes competed with her sister Vaughn Krieg Johnson an accomplished rodeo performer in her own right. Gene performed in trick riding events, relay races and bronc riding winning championships in several categories in Forth Worth, Chicago, New York's Madison Square Garden and the women's relay in Cheyenne in 1937. Unlike some of her peers she always rode slick, meaning the stirrups were not hobbled under the horse's belly.

Over the years both Creeds performed across the United States and Europe, Mexico and Australia eventually earning one of the highest honors rodeo offers, a lifetime membership in the Cowboy Hall of Fame. *From the private collection of Jack Davis, Olde America Antiques*

RUBY DICKEY

A very interesting card from the 1919 Tucumcari New Mexico Rodeo shows Ruby Dickey standing with her horse. On the reverse side is the following caption; "the girl that win (sic) the $300 prize riding bronks (sic)." Note that she wears her spurs buckled to the inside so that when sitting she merely places her right ankle on her left knee, and vice versa to unbuckle them.

This is one of the few examples where the split buttoned riding skirt is clearly seen. A flap of material starting from the waist could be buttoned on either side to form a full appearing skirt or a split style riding skirt. Few examples exist of this very functional piece of women's clothing. *Author's Collection*

VERNA DOBBS

RUTH DICKEY

From the 1916 Tucumcari New Mexico Round Up is a pose of Ruth Dickey on one of her relay horses. Note the switch she holds in her hand. An unusual image as this cowgirl is not wearing her hat but is wearing the long split riding skirt favored by the ladies in 1916. Is this Ruby's sister or is this the same cowgirl, nicknamed "Ruby"? *Author's Collection*

Many competing cowgirls at one time or another, traveled with various Wild West shows including Miller Brothers 101 Ranch. One of these performers for the 101 is Miss Verna Dobbs captured in a saucy pose complete with her leather fringed skirt, scalloped arm cuffs, classic scarf and peaked ten gallon hat. Not much is known about Miss Dobbs other than the fact that she did participate in the Wild West exhibition.

Other ladies who performed with the Wild West exhibition include Edith Barrington and Maude Jackson who are both listed in the "season of 1910" 101 Wild West Ranch program. They were hailed as being the most fearless and accomplished horsewomen in the world, and champion all-around cowgirls of the West. *Author's collection*

15

MILDRED DOUGLAS

In one of the rare wild steer contests captured in photo postcards, this one from the Cheyenne Frontier Days by Doubleday shows Mildred Douglas performing a grand ride.

Mildred's first relay race was in 1917 during Cheyenne where she rode C.B. Irwin horses which turned out to be their first race as well. It is reported that she once borrowed Lucille Mulhall's horse for her first trick riding competition at the Kansas City 1916 Stock Show after having been coached by Lucille.

Like many of her peers Mildred, too, went to Hollywood in 1917 where she worked in several films including *The Stage Coach Race*. It was here she met and married Pat Chrisman, trainer of *Tony*, Tom Mix's Wonder Horse. Hollywood never made her happy so she returned to the Wild West show and circus performances once appearing with the *Aristocratic Goats* as well as with a lion and some elephants. *Author's collection*

A very flashy dresser, Mildred Douglas was known for her fringed split skirts and vests. She rodeoed from 1916 to around 1926 participating in contests and performing, like her peers in most all of the exhibitions. While she survived many accidents including a broken ankle, arch and leg in separate accidents, amazingly she was never hurt riding broncs.

One of the few ladies born in the East, she learned to ride and jump at Minnie Thompson's indoor riding arena in Bridgeport, Connecticut. Leaving the formal schooling behind Mildred first worked in Barnum and Bailey's circus and later won bronc contests in Pendleton and Cheyenne among others. *Author's Collection*

FLORENCE FENTON

In this Doubleday photo is a clear, stop action image of Florence Fenton trick riding. Note her rubber soled riding shoes and the fancy saddle she is using.

Florence Fenton rode with the Tex Austin 1924 British Rodeo Exhibition which was produced at Wembley in conjunction with the British Empire Expedition. Tex, a well known and respected rodeo producer, had organized this trip to London in an effort to expose the rodeo sport to the British. Early rodeo, cowgirls, cowboys and western performers were at their zenith in the mid 20s and the Europeans were curious about this unique sport overtaking America. Even though several Wild West shows had been taken overseas earlier in the century, the rodeo presented a totally different aspect of America to the inquisitive Europeans. The Tex Austin 1924 British Rodeo Exhibition was remarkably well received paving the way for future shows in Europe as well as the Far East. *Wyoming State Museum*

BONNIE GRAY

Bonnie Gray was a foremost trick rider of her day who, in this Doubleday image is shown "going under" her horse, a feat which is as dangerous as it looks. Bonnie was one of the first ladies to master this crowd pleasing trick.

Bonnie once contracted to ride a bull in a Mexico exhibition but since the bull was trained for fighting and unfamiliar with having a rider on its back, she was nearly trampled to death.

Rodeo fans and Wild West aficionados were always delighted with the highly skilled trick riders. Often an exhibition was staged outside the show in an effort to attract more people to buy tickets to the event so they may see more tricks by the riders. Bonnie Gray rode her favorite horse *King Tut* on more than several occasions. In fact she so loved the animal that upon his death, she had a table made of his hide and four legs.

In one of the more famous episodes, *King Tut* caught his leg in a gopher hole just as he was about to perform his usual car jump. As a result, the publicity stunt got more than it bargained for. In a half-hearted manner, the horse continued his jump landing among a group of frightened viewers. Bonnie Gray tumbled over the terrified animal's head with her skirt caught on the saddle horn which gave the stunned crowd a full view of her undergarments. Thankfully she was liberated from her entangled skirt by an astute cowboy with a sharp knife. The humiliated cowgirl quickly exited the scene.

During her career as a movie stunt woman she doubled for most of the cowboy stars including Tim McCoy, Tom Mix, Hoot Gibson and Ken Maynard. Bonnie Gray was honored by the Cowgirl Hall of Fame in 1981. *Wyoming State Museum*

TOOTS GRIFFITH

Toots, one of the smaller cowgirls on the rodeo circuit, performs fancy or trick riding during the Parsons Round Up May, 1922. Note her flashy pinto, a color for horses which was just falling into favor due to their unusual, showy markings. As a rule, the working cowboys preferred not to use these uniquely marked horses; however, as the rodeo sport grew into exhibitions, the pintos were quickly recognized as crowd pleasers. *From the private collection of Jack Davis, Olde America Antiques*

The Griffith Trio included Toots Griffith, her husband Dean Griffith and their son who at the time was one of the youngest trick riders performing. Here they strut their stuff during the Parsons Round Up, May 1922 with both Toots and her son riding the preferred pinto horse, a favorite with the trick riders. *From the private collection of Jack Davis, Olde America Antiques*

REINE HAFLEY "WORLD'S GREATEST LADY TRICK RIDER."

During the August 1922 Monte Vista Round Up held in Colorado, Reine Hafley is shown in this Doubleday photo post card performing a death defying trick riding performance on her pinto. She was called the World's Greatest Lady Trick Rider, a title which once bestowed was held in perpetuity.

At one time she performed an act with an Arabian horse named *Lurline* during which she and the horse would jump 50 feet into a water tank. A highly successful stunt, she performed this jump twice a day, every day for weeks eventually earning enough money to purchase actress Lilly Langtree's private railroad car for a Wild West show. *From the private collection of Jack Davis, Olde America Antiques*

Most of the cowgirls performing and competing during the early years were proficient in many different rodeo events and Reine was no exception. Again at the Monte Vista Colorado Round Up she rides the bronc *Sleepy Jones*.

Reine Hafley, the daughter of pioneer Wild West showman Frank Hafley eloped with Dick Shelton during the summer of 1925 while he was performing with Miller Brothers 101 Ranch Wild West Show. She was a top bronc rider and trick rider winning the cowgirls' bronc riding contest in 1924 at Madison Square Garden. Reine Hafley Shelton was honored by the National Cowgirl Hall of Fame and Heritage Center in 1981. *Author's collection*

ELOISE FOX HASTINGS

Taken by Doubleday during the 1930 Houston Texas Show is a very fine image of Fox Hastings one of the very first female bulldoggers.

Born Eloise Fox, she ran away from her California home at the age of 14. Joining Irwin Brother's Wild West Show she performed trick and bronc riding on one of the fastest running trick riding horses performing at that time. After marrying bulldogger Mike Hastings, Eloise Fox dropped her first name joining her new last name with his becoming Fox Hastings. *Wyoming State Museum*

An unusual Doubleday image shows Fox Hastings performing her bulldogging event wearing a football helmet during a rodeo in Tucson, Arizona. The use of protective body gear of any kind was almost unheard of during the early years of rodeo which makes this a unique photo.

Bulldogging was introduced by black cowboy Bill Pickett who, in the act of wrestling down the rangy steer, bit the animal's lip. Reportedly his boss commented that Bill was a regular "Bulldog" holding the steer with his teeth. Now termed Steer Wrestling, few still bite the steer's lip. Because of this act, Pickett was contracted by Miller's 101 Ranch becoming a headliner there. Some dispute still remains as to who truly invented bulldogging/steer wrestling; however, due to the publicity Bill Pickett received with the 101 Ranch Show, he is generally given the credit. *From the private collection of Jack Davis, Olde America Antiques*

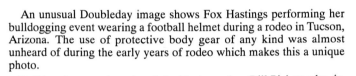
HASTINGS BULLDOGGING TUCSON ARIZ.

This Doubleday image of Fox Hastings taken during the Pendleton Round Up, shows this remarkable lady bulldogging a steer.

As a rule, the bulldogging events held with cowgirls was generally an exhibition rather than a competition. Performing this exhibition of the event, she is listed in the Round Up souvenir program from Pendleton, dated Thursday September 17, 1925 as the world's only lady bulldogger. Hasting's first show of bulldogging was in 1924 in Beaumont, California. With encouragement and instruction from her husband, himself a highly successful bulldogger, she evolved foremost in this field. *Author's collection*

An action scene by Doubleday with the rodeo unidentified, Fox Hastings is shown on *Hair Trigger*, a highly animated bucking bronc. It appears that the stirrups are hobbled, tied together under the belly of the horse. One can almost hear that horse squeal! *Wyoming State Museum*

This is a rare triple image showing Fox Hastings in her familiar studio pose, riding her favorite horse and performing the rodeo exhibition of bulldogging. *Wyoming State Museum*

Fox Hastings waves to the cameraman, Doubleday as she performs her famous bulldogging event during the 1930 Houston Rodeo. She is wearing the same striped blouse, now very muddy, that she wore in the studio poses taken earlier by Doubleday. Note the wall-eyed expression on the steer who also appears to have protective caps on its horns. *Author's Collection*

Here Fox strikes a lovely pose in the studio of Doubleday. This image is another desirable card as it is a close up of an identified cowgirl, plus the title of "Lady Champion Bulldogger" has been lettered onto the negative.

Sadly, in 1948, Fox Hastings took her life in a Phoenix, Arizona hotel. *Wyoming State Museum*

DORIS HAYNES

Stryker was known for his unusual angles used in photographing rodeo personalities which, in this case, causes the viewer to believe the animal is truly airborne. It was during the mid 1940s that Stryker published his postcards using what he called the "photogloss system," which was simply a glossy finish much like what is used today.

In this image from his rodeo series 5, Doris Haynes rides the bronc *Brown Derby*. A friend of Gene Creed, Doris rode broncs in Australia for one of their rodeo expositions. *Author's Collection*

PRAIRIE ROSE HENDERSON

Known simply as Prairie Rose, this colorful cowgirl was recognized for her flashy outfits many of which were comprised of fancy beaded leather with lots of fringe and sometimes feathers or sequins. Here she poses with her horse at the Cheyenne Frontier Days Rodeo in a D.F.P. Co. Inc. image which is a Doubleday card. The initials stand for Doubleday Frontier Photo Company, Inc. *Wyoming State Museum*

Seen in the distance, near the fence is Prairie Rose riding a bronc at the Toppenish Round Up in 1914. A rare, early card identifying the location, the cowgirl and the date.

Rose was born Ann Robbins either in the 1870s or perhaps as late as 1890, the exact date has never been known. Her name *Prairie Rose* supposedly came from the Wyoming prairie with Henderson the name of her first husband. She had several husbands including Johnny Judd, Charles Coleman and a fellow named Larson.

An early day performer, she rode as early as 1906 eventually becoming declared one of the all-time great winners excelling as a bronc rider. By 1911 she was awarded the title of Champion and started riding for C.B. Irwin. *Author's Collection*

A rare photo postcard by Marcell shows Prairie Rose on the bronc named *Idaho* during the Pioneer Days in Vancouver, Washington.

In 1917, The Union Pacific Railroad presented her with a large silver belt buckle for bronc riding after being declared the Champion in Cheyenne, Wyoming. Bronc riding was not her only specialty as she participated in numerous flat races the first 10 years of rodeoing. *Author's Collection*

During the Pendleton Round Up, Prairie Rose rides as number 33 on the bronc *Brown Jug*.

The Second Annual Round Up *She's Wild* held in Bozeman, Montana listed Prairie Rose in the program as a contestant for "event No. 7 - Lady's Broncho Riding Contest for Friday August 6, 1920." In that same program the following Cowgirls are listed for the bucking event; Red Bird, Mrs. Eugene Hall, Lorena Trickey, Ruth Roach and Kitty Canutt. *Author's Collection*

PRAIRIE ROSE HENDERSON ON "I'M GONE" "STAMPEDE" NEW YORK CITY 1916

Prairie Rose rides the bronc *I'm Gone* during the New York City 1916 Stampede. This is a rare photo postcard taken by Newman as it shows the date, location, and the cowgirl's name. Not many Newman photos can be found.

On the reverse of this card is the following message sent home by an attendee..."This afternoon the champion rider was thrown. This girl wins the title. One fellow broke his collarbone and another broke his leg within a few feet of my seat." *Author's Collection*

PRAIRIE ROSE
(PEBCO)

This Doubleday photo exemplifies Prairie Rose Henderson's unusual outfits. A sad ending for this popular cowgirl came sometime in 1930s when she left her ranch home in a blizzard, possibly to tend to the animals and became lost. Years later her body was found reportedly identified only by her large championship silver belt buckle. *Author's Collection*

HELEN KIRKENDALL

A very rare and desirable image by DeVere Helfrich of Klamath Falls, Oregon who used the professional name of simply DeVere. On the reverse side of this photo postcard is the following: "A 'Natural-Finish' Card Made by Graycraft Card Co., Danville, Va."

In this late card Helen Kirkendall rides the bronc *June Bug* at the Roseburg Oregon Rodeo in 1945. *Author's Collection*

JOELLA IRWIN

One of three daughters of legendary C.B. Irwin, Joella was an outstanding relay rider. With her father producing shows from coast to coast and even in Canada, Joella and her sisters were born into rodeo. C.B. is recognized as having influenced the rodeo business more than any other individual and as such was instrumental in organizing the Cheyenne Frontier Days.

Joella is shown here in this Doubleday photo with an unusually marked Appaloosa horse complete with a beautiful hand tooled, silver studded saddle.

In 1916 show promoter Guy Weadick contracted with C.B. Irwin to supply stock for his gigantic New York Stampede. It is widely known that on opening day Joella was bucked off about six times over the course of the track during the relay race. Because she persevered, eventually ending the race last, the judges awarded her a $500 cash prize just for hanging on! *Author's Collection*

MISS BILLIE KING.

BILLIE KING

Included in this collection because of its clarity, this photo of Billie King was probably not taken by Doubleday simply because he generally indicated his copyright notice on the face of his images. Yet the handwriting appears to be Doubleday's.

Note her beautiful inlaid boots. Not much is known about Billie except that she appeared at a King Brothers Rodeo and was listed with Pauline Lovenze, Dorothy Barden, Violet Corathan, Margie Henson, Alice Greenough, Violet Clements and Skeeter Bix. Unfortunately the date, place or additional details about this lovely cowgirl are lost to time. *Author's Collection*

BEA KIRNAN

A smiling Bea Kirnan poses for this Doubleday photo. Just prior to participating in the 1916 Guy Weadick's New York Sheepshead Bay Stampede, Bea Brossard married Tommy Kirnan, an intensely dedicated cowboy considered by many as the best of all time. Bea is listed along with other trick riders Tilly Baldwin, Lottie Vondreau and Peggy Warren. Both Bea and Tommy won parts of their various events in spite of the fact that this was his first contest rodeo.

Both Kirnan's were part of the 1924 Tex Austin London rodeo Exhibition at Wembley. In an effort to constantly promote the show, Tex Austin show performers were requested to don their colorful western togs at all times. Often Bea wore a fancy crimson roping outfit with silk sash and white tie.

The Kirnan's put together a theater rodeo act which played at the London Coliseum after the successful Tex Austin show. They called themselves "Tommy Kirnan Presents Wembley Rodeo." Traveling from London to Dublin Ireland, to Paris and Brussels they performed their rodeo acts to packed houses of enthusiastic Europeans. Several of the other rodeo performers who worked with Austin stayed on with the Kirnans.

It was with this 1924 exhibition that Bea rode a terrific trick riding horse *Rubio* which was given to her during a show in Argentina, South America. *Author's Collection*

TAD BARNES LUCAS

One of the best known cowgirls, Tad Lucas, is shown in this Doubleday postcard where she is riding a wild steer during the Aurora, Colorado Fair.

Tad Lucas, 1902-1989, was born Barbara Barnes. Her father nicknamed her "Tadpole" which was eventually shortened to Tad, the name she used for the rest of her life. On her Nebraska family ranch she rode calves at a very early age being egged on by her older brothers. Later she rode bucking horses in the town square of Cody, Nebraska.

Tad's first contest was in 1916 during Gordon Nebraska County Fair at the tender age of 14. Here, an advertisement for girls' steer riding contest gave the young cowgirl her first win of day money and finals with both her challengers being bucked off.

By 1920 she joined California Frank Hafley's Wild West Show traveling for the first time into Mexico City, Guadalajara and Pueblo. Over this time period she developed an interest in trick riding, and bucking horses.

Just prior to boarding the S.S. Menominee for England with the Tex Austin Troupe, she married Buck Lucas, All Around Cowboy and horse trainer. Immediately upon their return from England they spent some time with the 101 Wild West Show, moving to Fort worth in 1925.

She won the All Around Champion Cowgirl in New York in both 1928 and 1930 and won trick riding at Cheyenne 6 times, even though this was her least favorite event.

Tad Lucas suffered a severely shattered arm during a trick riding accident in 1933 at the Chicago World's Fair when she was riding her favorite trick horse, a black gelding named *Candylamb*. Her arm was in the cast for about 3 years. Performing in 1935 at Madison Square Garden with her arm still in a cast was exciting for the fans because Tad figured the cast just slowed her down a little, but did not stop her performing.

She was the undisputed champion trick rider from 1925 to 1933 with her celebrated back drag being the highlight of her performance. She would arch her back over the horse's rear hanging her head just shy of the pounding hooves of the galloping horse in a death defying act! *Wyoming State Museum*

Tad Lucas on "Hell Cat"

© R. R. DOUBLEDAY
12AT303

One of the scarce, collectible linen post cards as photographed by Doubleday, shows Tad Lucas on the bronc *Hell Cat.* Note her woolly chaps popular in the mid 1940s with the ladies.

Success became her middle name with performances in all 48 states, Australia, Canada, England and more. She was named All-Around Cowgirl at Madison Square Garden's world championship rodeo a total of 8 times and awarded permanent ownership of the $10,000 trophy given by Metro-Goldwyn-Mayer for three consecutive victories there. In 1938, Gordon, Nebraska had proclaimed August 31 Tad Lucas Day.

Tad Lucas was a member of one of the last European or overseas trips a rodeo troupe would take which was for the 1958 Belgium World's Fair. Upon arriving in Brussels the travel money was not available as promised leaving about 150 American rodeo performers abandoned. Eventually they did return home using a plane offered by the US Embassy.

Always a leader, Tad Lucas was hailed as founding a new style of pants for cowgirls. In the late 1920s she stitched colorful patches of cloth into or along the seam of the flare of the bell bottomed slacks similar to those worn by the Mexican Wild West riders. Rhinestones and sequins could now also be found sewn onto the bell bottomed trousers. This style replaced the jodhpurs but by the 40s many cowgirls would be seen wearing the familiar denim jeans.

With her husband Buck, they produced rodeos in later years and owned a bucking horse string. *Author's Collection*

Tad Lucas competed in rodeo longer than any other cowgirl; here while on horseback, she holds her daughter Mitzi.

Appearing in Ripley's Believe It or Not she was pictured as a trick-riding grandmother as her daughter and granddaughter both pursued trick-riding careers.

For several performances at the Kansas City Rodeo, Tad even helped a clown act during which she would appear to be a fan seated in the grandstand taunting the working clowns. Totally annoyed, the clowns would drag the 'fan' out of her seat and stuff her into the barrel right before the charging bull. Even though she suffered multiple bruises, she still enjoyed the 'fun' of rodeo.

Tad Lucas was honored by the National Cowboy Hall of Fame in 1968, by the Cowgirl Hall of Fame in 1978 and in 1979 honored by the Professional Rodeo Cowgirls Hall of Fame in Colorado Springs, Colorado. *Author's Collection*

29

BONNIE McCARROLL

Taken at the Pendleton Round Up by Doubleday is Bonnie Mc Carroll posing with her horse without a saddle. Note the headstall which appears to have some horsehair parts, popular during the heyday of the cowgirl. Note, too, the horse's split ear!

Bonnie is wearing silky bloomers which were probably red, white stockings and what appears to be colorful stitched boots with a deep scallop pointing to a heart. Around the top of her boots are the four suits of playing cards, a popular design of the period. *Wyoming State Museum*

Bonnie Mc Carroll performed during the Aurora Colorado Fair and as demonstrated in the Doubleday photo postcard, she more than likely did not stay aboard this wild steer. *Wyoming State Museum*

This Pendleton Association photo shows Bonnie Mc Carroll during the celebrated Oregon Round Up on the bronc *Tango* a famous horse from the Cliff King string named after popular dance steps.

Bonnie is also listed in the Official Souvenir Program from Pendleton dated 1925 as an exhibition rider for the Cowgirl's Bucking Contest riding *Billie Buck*. *Author's Collection*

Reproduced numerous times in many books, this now infamous photo postcard by W.S. Bowman shows Bonnie Mc Carroll thrown from the bronc *Silver* after her hobbled stirrup strap broke during the Pendleton Round Up.

Perhaps this was a prophecy into the future as 14 years later Bonnie, unable to free herself from the hobbles, was violently whipped back and forth on a Pendleton bronc causing fatal injuries. She died eight days after the horrific ride. It is believed that her tragic death was the end to ladies bronc competition in 1929. *Author's Collection*

VERA McGINNIS

Fancy beaded leather gauntlets, fringed leather skirts, large hair bows and colorful neck scarves complete the outfits for the day in this postcard image of Vera Mc Ginnis taken during the 1916 *Passing of the West* series of rodeos held that summer. This particular view was during the Billings, Montana show. Vera had been offered $100 per week by organizer Mr. C.L. Harris to travel and perform trick riding while husband Earl Simpson would be able to compete in the open events held during the series of rodeos.

Discovering rodeo through an old hand and movie actor Art Acord, she eventually earned the title of the cowgirl rider to beat. Her exciting rodeo career was launched in Salt Lake Utah during the Frontier Day Celebration held on the 4th of July 1913. Even though she placed third in the relay race, Vera was nevertheless bitten by the rodeo bug. She quit her office job to pursue her newly found career.

By 1914, "Mac" a nick name given her by Art Acord, won Roman standing race at Pendleton. The prize for winning the relay race at Idaho Falls was a hand carved, silver mounted saddle and a cartridge belt with matching holster. Later Smith and Wesson gave her a .22 for that holster.

Vera won the relay race during the Rogue River Round Up in 1918. In addition to the relay races, over the course of her career she rode broncs, wild steers, raced Roman, rode bucking bulls and performed trick riding exhibitions. *Author's Collection*

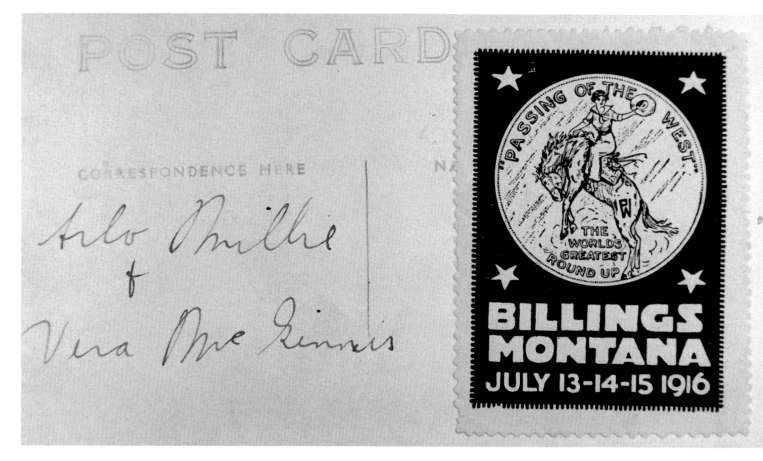

Shown here is the reverse side of the previous photo onto which has been stuck the famous "Passing of the West" sticker which was available for each of the various Montana locations. A series of round ups held in the state celebrated many well-known performers and rodeo contestants. These stickers are very rare and highly collectible. *Author's Collection*

A rare W.S. Bowman photo postcard shows Vera Mc Ginnis in the "drunken ride" during the Pendleton Round Up.

Her fascinating career veered off into Hollywood while her husband reported for duty with Uncle Sam in 1917. Stunt doubling in several movies did not satisfy this rodeo professional so she left the glitter of Hollywood for her own Rodeo Road. By summer of 1919 she was contracted by Jim Parsons to ride the relay races for him during the Calgary Canada Stampede during which she won her largest purse to date of $1,000 for first prize.

For a very short time in 1923 she actually worked for the Greatest Show on Earth, where she performed her trick riding. After the circus closed she quickly returned to rodeoing. Vera Mc Ginnis traveled the world including Hawaii, Japan and Europe during her rodeo career.

The evolution of the relay race eventually removed the requirement for the cowgirls to re-saddle each horse in their string. With this action eliminated, in 1923 Vera literally invented the flying change during the race, that of actually jumping from one horse to the next without hitting the ground. Perhaps this is the reason why she won two events, the relay race and the women's trick riding during the 1924 Tex Austin Show in London. Vera did stay on after the Austin Show closed to tour Europe and perform with a small group of rodeo hands.

Earning a livelihood by performing at various rodeos and round ups kept Vera busy through the twenties and early 1930s. During a wild relay race in 1934 Vera almost lost her life as a result of a terrible accident during which her horse fell on top of her. Vera never called it an accident but rather an experience. She survived a collapsed lung, broken ribs, five broken lumbar vertebrae in her back and a broken right hip, not to mention a broken neck. The prognosis was not favorable as she was not given any chance of living and if she did survive, would be a cripple for the rest of her life.

Not accepting either prediction, Vera underwent painful procedures to mend her seriously broken body. A short six months after the accident Vera was able to ride *Tiny*, her last trick-riding horse. She would not be a cripple!

Vera Mc Ginnis was one of the three foremost pioneer rodeo cowgirls to be inducted into the Rodeo Hall of Fame in Oklahoma City in 1975. One year prior to her induction she wrote *Rodeo Road My Life as a Pioneer Cowgirl*, a fascinating book on her life on the rodeo circuit. *From the private collection of Jack Davis, Olde America Antiques*

DOROTHY MORRELL

Dated 1920 this is a lovely view of Dorothy Morrell on her trick riding horse. Note the fancy silver saddle with the extra long tapaderos. Another rare card as it is autographed by Dorothy making it highly collectible and desirable.

It was during the Pendleton Round Up in 1914 that Dorothy was judged World's Champion Cowgirl Bronc Rider, a title which she kept for life. *Author's Collection*

This extremely interesting photograph taken during the Clayton New Mexico Rodeo shows Dorothy Morrell winning her first prize money. What makes this rare is that the rodeo photographer can be seen on the far left of the image, it could be Doubleday himself! *Author's Collection*

DOROTHY MORRELL RIDING 'CRAWFISH' ALLIANCE, RODEO,

During the Alliance, Nebraska rodeo, Dorothy Morrell rode the bronc *Crawfish* as shown in this Doubleday photo postcard. *Wyoming State Museum*

This is an unusual image taken by photographer Trout during the Salinas California Rodeo. Dorothy Morrell has somehow managed to fall off a seemingly placid burro. The story needs to be known on this scene.

The Wild Bunch, a newsletter which was published by the Rodeo Hall of Fame noted that Dorothy Morrell won the medal for World's Champion All-Around Cowgirl along with winning the title of the World's Best Cowgirl Bronk (sic) Rider. Medals were presented to her on what was known as *Movie Day* held during the New York Guy Weadick Rodeo in 1917. Previous to these honors she was elected Queen of the Panama Pacific International Exposition in San Francisco being presented with a beautiful gold watch. It was also reported in this newsletter, that Dorothy was one of several performers who were injured during Weadick's contest. By this date she had already married Skeeter Bill Robbins. *From the private collection of Jack Davis, Olde America Antiques*

DOROTHY MORRELL ON PINTO PETE
CHEYENNE FRONTIER DAYS.

This is an incredible action photo postcard of Dorothy Morrell on *Pinto Pete* taken by Doubleday in 1926 during the Cheyenne Frontier Days. A magnificent pose on an animated, classic bucking horse, this image has been printed numerous times in many publications as it typifies the beautiful cowgirl on a wild bronc. *Author's Collection*

LUCILLE MULHALL

Photographer Marcell captured Lucille Mulhall, Champion Lady Steer Roper of the World, in a classic 1914 pose with her horse. Daughter of Col. Zack Mulhall, founder and owner of Mulhall's Wild West Show, Lucille was the first lady to be called a *cowgirl*. This title was bestowed upon her by none other than Will Rogers after he saw her first public appearance in 1899 St. Louis during her father's Roping and Riding Contest. *Author's Collection*

Lucille is shown in a rare image roping a cowboy on a galloping horse.

Termed *roping and riding contests* in the early days, these gatherings of ranch hands evolved into Wild West shows and eventually rodeos. Col. Zack Mulhall's daughter Lucille was only 14 years old when she performed with the group of Mulhall's *Congress of Rough Riders and Ropers*. She won the roping contest being awarded $1,000 by roping and tying three different steers in 30 to 45 second time frames.

Termed Champion Lady Rider and Roper of the World as early as 1903, Lucille performed in Wild West shows and competed in rodeos through the mid 1940s. *From the private collection of Jack Davis, Olde America Antiques*

Up against the fence is the steer roped by Lucille Mulhall during the Walla Walla Washington 1914 Frontier Days. Money was tight and it is believed that Lucille chose to appear in this rodeo between theater engagements in order to maintain a positive cash flow. Unfortunately there is no record of her winning in Walla Walla.

Photographed by Marcell, the official photographer, this is a rare, clear image of the famous Lady Champion Roper of the World. Note that she is wearing a long, split riding skirt. Note too, that she has only one leather cuff to protect her left arm from rope burns. *From the private collection of Jack Davis, Olde America Antiques*

Lucille Mulhall is shown in this postcard on one of her trick horses *Eddie C.*. Note her fancy saddle with the long tapaderos. The year was 1915 and Lucille was just 29 years old with her first booking for the year at the Cosy Theater in Okmulgee, Oklahoma. During the next several years the theater and rodeo performances seemed to be back to back as she capitalized on her talents with rope and horse. *Author's Collection*

Prior to the Sheridan Stampede held in September 1915, the Denver Post had given Lucille Mulhall a tremendous amount of publicity. When she appeared in Sheridan, her horse had been named *The Denver Post* when in all likelihood it was still *Eddie C.*. *Author's Collection*

In a rare, behind the scenes type of moment, Lucille Mulhall is leading one of her horses. The *World's first titled cowgirl* retired from the theater and rodeo in 1922 returning to the family homestead in Mulhall, Oklahoma. Just two months after her 55th birthday in 1940, Lucille was killed in an automobile accident. Lucille Mulhall was inducted into the Rodeo Hall of Fame December 1975. *Author's Collection*

PEGGY MURRAY

During the Sarasota Rodeo held in Florida, Doubleday caught trick rider Peggy Murray in a difficult action which takes a tremendous amount of balance and coordination not to mention physical fitness. Note the pinto horse favored by many of the trick or fancy riders. *From the private collection of Jack Davis, Olde America Antiques*

RUTH PARTON

At the tender age of 17, local girl Ruth Parton performed in the relay race at the Toppenish Washington Round Up. Legend has it that C.B. Irwin refused to allow the tardy participant to compete against his daughters by literally holding shut the entrance gate. Undaunted, Ruth's father Bert Parton purchased a string of fine thoroughbred horses for his daughter. *Author's Collection*

One of the more artful poses taken by photographer Bawgus is Ruth Parton Champion Relay Rider of the World. Her number 77 clearly shows pinned to the back of her buckskin shirt. Note her beaded and fringed buckskin gauntlets and high peaked Stetson hat. *Author's Collection*

Ruth Parton
Champion Relay
Rider of the World

(Photo By Bawgus Wi-W-Wa.)

Here is a very uncommon photo postcard showing the various trophies won by rodeo contestant famed relay rider Ruth Parton who is holding her #1 thoroughbred horse. Her magnificent silver trophy is flanked by the saddles and other booty won by racing in the relay. Reportedly she was so accomplished that C.B. Irwin offered her a position in his relay team which she accepted eventually riding with Irwin from Canada to Mexico. *Author's Collection*

FLORENCE HUGHES RANDOLPH

This is a lovely photo taken late in her career of Florence Hughes Randolph who gained fame in 1919 during the Calgary Stampede when she won the Roman race competing against men.

Florence left home to join a small traveling Wild West show at the age of 14. Early in her career Florence Hughes performed in the circus eventually forming her own Wild West show which she called Princess Mohawk's Wild West Hippodrome. Because of her spreading fame in this endeavor she was often listed as *Princess Mohawk* on the contestant rosters.

Known as an outstanding performer in trick riding and broncs, she won the ladies' bronc riding event in 1926 at Philadelphia's Sesqui-Centennial Rodeo. Victories were taken also in Chicago, New York and St. Louis. A spin in Hollywood included some stunt doubling for name actresses where she rode her horse down steep inclines or jumped them over obstacles or ditches. Her attractiveness was celebrated by Mack Sennett as he selected her as one of his bathing beauties.

Her favorite horse was a chestnut and white paint she called *Boy*. Florence Hughes married Floyd Randolph a Wild West showman, rodeo man, sheriff and saddle shop owner, in 1925.

During her later years, she helped produce and manage the Ardmore Rodeo held annually in Oklahoma. Florence Hughes Randolph was honored by the National Cowboy Hall of fame in 1968. *From the private collection of Jack Davis, Olde America Antiques*

Ruth Parton is shown here around 1917 with her string of thoroughbred horses and is termed Champion Lady Relay Rider of the World. Note the same beaded gauntlets she wore in a previous photo. *Author's Collection*

LUCYLE RICHARDS BULLDOGGING AR...
COPYRIGHT R.R. DOUBLEDAY

LUCYLE ROBERTS RICHARDS

This is a rare head-on view by Doubleday, of cowgirl Lucyle Roberts Richards bulldogging at an Ardmore Oklahoma Rodeo.

Like most of these pioneering women cowgirls, Lucyle's career was most exciting. Not only was she an accomplished rodeo performer, she also achieved status as a recognized air acrobat executing over a dozen tricks including the Immelman, the Lazy S and the Falling Leaf. According to Lucyle, acrobatic flying was just like trick riding "All you do is keep your head and dash into it--careless like."

Lucyle began her rodeo career at age 13 by riding bucking steers and bucking horses eventually touring with various wild west shows, including the famed 101 Ranch, and rodeos throughout the 20s and 30s. Winning the World Champion Saddle Bronc Riding Competition in Chicago, 1930 and again in Boston, 1934 she also took first place in trick riding at Henderson, Texas and placed second in saddle bronc riding in London.

Her aviation career took off in 1939 when during WWII Lucyle ferried bombers over to England. Lucyle Roberts Richards was honored in 1987 by the National Cowgirl Hall of Fame. *Wyoming State Museum*

RUTH ROACH

Again, here is one of those terrific Doubleday poses taken during the 1930 Houston Show. This is Ruth Roach, the darling of the rodeo circuit. Note her beautifully stitched boots, silk blouse, high "Stetson" and large hair bow.

Ruth Roach performed in the Circus before pursuing a career in rodeo. She also was a participant in the 1914 European Miller's 101 Ranch Show tour. During a very colorful career, Ruth rode bronc riding exhibitions in 1917 in Fort Worth, Texas, plus she rode *Searchlight* a notorious bronc at the Chicago Stadium in 1927. *Wyoming State Museum*

RUTH ROACH

(DOUBLEDAY) PHOTO

Many of the cowgirls maintained a menagerie of pets including the usual horses and dogs; however, Ruth Roach kept a spotted pig for a time. In this Doubleday image Ruth is shown feeding her special little friend. Note she is wearing the same boots she wore during the Houston Show.

Winning the Cowgirl's Bronc Riding at "World Series Rodeo," Madison Square Garden in 1932 Ruth Roach's prize included a magnificent hand tooled saddle. *Author's Collection*

RUTH ROACH

(© DOUBLEDAY)

In one of the early Doubleday images Ruth Roach appears in a classic cowgirl pose with her best fringed outfit and her favorite horse.

One year, just prior to the rodeo activities, the lobby of the Hotel Texas in Forth Worth became the scene of some trick riding by Ruth Roach as an enticement to attract ticket buying fans in order to see the balance of her act. Like many of her contemporaries, she was a multi talented performer believing that if a girl could mount a horse she was therefore capable of trick riding. *Author's Collection*

Ruth Roach is shown in the Doubleday image during the 1920 Cheyenne Wyoming Frontier Days being titled the Lady Champion Bronc Rider.

In an effort to win more money, most cowgirls entered multiple contests at the same rodeo. She is listed in the 1920 Bozeman Montana Rodeo program for "event number 7 Lady's broncho contest riding *Sage Hen*."

After Tex Austin's traveling rodeo completed a rewarding tour of England and Europe in 1924, Ruth Roach was part of a small troupe who remained performing on stage at London's Coliseum Theater. Others who stayed on were Bea Kirnan, Vera Roberts and Vera McGinnis along with 5 cowboys. Comprised of the usual rodeo feats including bronc riding, trick riding and racing, their stage was shared with jugglers, dancers and a high-wire act. *Author's Collection*

MILDRED ROGERS

Here is the Queen of the Round Up from Pendleton, Oregon in 1925. This photo postcard was taken by a photographer for Pendleton Drug Company who published thousands of postcards just for the rodeo. *From the private collection of Jack Davis, Olde America Antiques*

HELEN RUE

JOSIE SEDGWICK

During the Tri-State Round Up held at Belle Fourche, South Dakota photographer Doubleday captured Helen Rue rearing her horse in what appears to be an awkward pose for the animal. *Author's Collection*

Another Pendleton Drug Company image of the 1924 Queen of the Round Up, Josie Sedgwick, taken at Pendleton, Oregon. *Author's Collection*

ROSE SMITH

Just after removing the blindfold from this bronc, Rose Smith unfortunately takes a bad fall from the confused animal in this Doubleday postcard. Hailed as one of the famous female bronc riders in the 1920s Rose Smith often competed with all the top cowgirls on the rodeo circuit. *Author's Collection*

Rose Smith was a multi-talented cowgirl as is indicated in this Doubleday card where she is shown trick riding on her pinto horse. The stand she is performing looks awkward with the bow legged effect but should she straighten her legs, she would slide right back down onto the saddle! Rose was married to Oklahoman Curly Roberts. *Author's Collection*

Rose Smith Riding High on Easy Money

Stryker's "Photogloss"–Rodeo Series - 3

Action scenes are rare and desirable especially when the cowgirl is identified or the rodeo location and horse are named.

Here, in this Doubleday postcard, Rose Smith on the bucking horse *Banjo* ends up over the fence and is ruled out. If only Doubleday had taken a sequence of photos during the next 2 minutes! Note her contestant's number on her right elbow. *Wyoming State Museum*

An amazing angle for a bronc has been captured by Stryker in his rodeo series 3 with his special processing called "Photogloss." Here Rose Smith takes flight on the bronc *Easy Money*. On the reverse is the following hand-written note: "May 6, 1945 Dear Grandmom, This is a picture of the rodeo in Feb. 1944 that daddy got last year. It doesn't look real but it is...." Mailed from Tucson, Arizona in 1945 it is still a penny postcard. *Author's Collection*

FANNIE SPERRY STEELE

Fannie's earliest work in her now famous career came in 1904 when she was sponsored by the Capital Stock and Food Company in Helena to ride in women's relay races in Helena, Butte, Anaconda and Missoula. These races, copied from the earlier wild west shows were a terrific hit with the fans and Fannie enjoyed every minute of the competition. Additionally she was one of the first women invited to participate in the 1912 Calgary Stampede.

It was during 1913 that she met and married W.S. Bill Steele who competed as a bronc rider and worked as a rodeo clown with the trademark of dressing like Uncle Sam. Together they rodeoed all over the country and performed with the Miller Brother's and Irwin Wild West Shows.

A year after their marriage, while they were performing at the Miles City Rodeo in 1914, Fannie and Bill organized their *Powder River Wild West Show* which became a profitable venture for the headlining pair.

The year before this photo was taken, Fannie Sperry Steele also won the Calgary 1912 Stampede earning the title of Woman Saddle Bronc Riding Champion of the World. Here in this Marcell photo is Fannie competing during the Winnipeg Stampede of 1913.

Travelling and rodeoing proved successful for the Steele's yet between 1917 and 1919 the couple accepted only the Montana rodeos. By 1919 they purchased land near Helena settling down to ranch life. As Bill's health began to fail, Fannie made the decision to retire after 20 years as a rodeo performer appearing for the last time at the Bozeman Round Up in 1925.

Bill Steele died in 1939 after which Fannie worked as an outfitter and guide from her ranch in Helmville, Montana. *Author's Collection*

A rare photo postcard shows Fannie Sperry Steele on the bronc *Snowball* during the Windham Round Up held in Miles City, Montana late August 1920.

This native of Montana was one of the most dedicated to her profession of all her counterparts. Growing up on a ranch where she and her mother were the only true horse lovers, Fannie acquired a love for the animal. As a result of her confidence around horses, Fannie never rode hobbled, she always rode slick (the stirrups were loose, not tied under the horse's belly), a fact which drew attention from the press as well as from the rodeo fans. It was once reported that the women who rode slick were few in number and included the likes of Tillie Baldwin, Bertha Blancett, Nettie Hawn, and of course Fannie Sperry Steele. *Author's Collection*

MABEL DeLONG STRICKLAND

In this postcard, produced by the Pendleton Drug Company, Mabel Strickland is performing a steer roping exhibition. Note her outstretched arms which eventually became her trademark. See too, that she is wearing her favorite pair of boots with the four suits from a deck of cards along the top edge. *Author's Collection*

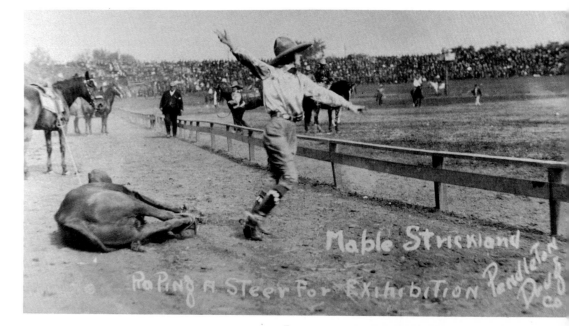

Mabel Strickland poses for photographer Doubleday, with some of her ropes hung on the protective fence. Note her colorful satin blouse and neckerchief. Her sash is probably a brilliant hue as well. Again, Mabel wears her favorite boots.

It was during her victorious years at Cheyenne that Mabel DeLong married rodeo cowboy Hugh Strickland, one of the best all around cowboys. He successfully taught this able cowgirl steer roping which she eventually perfected into a contract exhibition. Advertising their combined rodeo talents in various entertainment publications such as The Billboard, their appearance at a rodeo guaranteed an outstanding contest not only with regard to fan attendance, but often with the promoters as Hugh Strickland would assist in directing the arena if needed. *Author's Collection, courtesy of Howdyshell Photos, Oregon*

This truly lovely postcard image of Mabel Strickland taken by Doubleday is a another ideal studio pose for the cowgirl. Mabel was, without question, the most beloved cowgirl in early rodeo. Had official rodeo records been kept prior to 1929, Mabel would have won more world titles than any of her contemporaries. A talented, poised, confident, qualified rodeo performer and contestant, Mabel Strickland was the cowgirl's cowgirl. *Author's Collection*

No photo postcard collection on cowgirls of the golden west would be complete without this image taken by Doubleday during the Pendleton Round Up. Perhaps the most famous picture of a cowgirl ever taken is of Mabel Strickland in her trademark pose after roping and tying a steer. Arms outstretched, perched on one foot, Mabel signals to the time keeper she has accomplished her feat. A highly desirable, collectible photo postcard.

Mabel Strickland is featured on the cover of the 1926 Frontier Days souvenir program riding *Stranger* which is the only time in the history of the Round Up that a cowgirl graced its cover. *Author's Collection*

TRICKLAND CHAMPION LADY TRICK RIDER,
(DOUBLEDAY)   BELL-FOURCHE S.DAK.

An exciting action scene of Mabel Strickland, Champion Lady Trick Rider where she performs in front of the spectator stands in Belle Fourche, South Dakota. Here she executes her flawless act on a snow-white Arabian mare; however, her favorite horse was *Buster*, a thoroughbred who was much respected by race horsemen and ropers. This Doubleday image provides the collector with what the rodeo stands and flavor must have been.

This 1981 Cowboy Hall of Fame Honoree was born Mabel DeLong in Wallula on the Columbia River in Washington State in 1897. At the age of 13, she began her rodeo career by relay racing in Walla Walla, Washington riding with the Drumhellers, horsemen and rodeo producers. Enjoying a wonderful string of blooded horses for her relay mounts, Mabel quickly became a highly respected competitor among her peers. Possessing an uncommon ability to get the most wind out of her relay string, Mabel won the championship twice in the 1920s at Cheyenne and won five years and placed second five years at Pendleton from 1916 to 1923. *Wyoming State Museum*

STRICKLAND ROPING AT TRIANGL
(DOUBLEDAY)

able Strickland
Queen
of the Pendleton
Round Up
1927

Without a doubt Mabel Strickland was the most highly photographed cowgirl in her time. Here she is titled the Queen of the Pendleton Round Up 1927 in this Pendleton Drug Company postcard.

For her turn in the movies, she had a bit part in *Rhythm of the Range* with Bing Crosby. She also did what was called "replacement riding," or what we now call stunt work for actresses in the Hollywood movies. *From the private collection of Jack Davis, Olde America Antiques*

Mabel Strickland is shown here in the Doubleday card roping at the Triangle R Ranch.

A petite cowgirl she perfected numerous rodeo skills including steer riding, bronc riding, trick riding and steer roping, even riding bulls during the Tucumcari New Mexico Round Up. It has been reported that Mabel and Lucille Mulhall were the first early women who roped and busted steers. She once roped, tripped and tied a steer in 18 seconds flat at the Pendleton Round Up. Mabel's career was enviable as she won consecutive championships in trick riding in Walla Walla in 1913, 1914 and 1915.

Because of a short contestant list, the arena director in Fort Worth, 1917, volunteered Mabel to the bucking horse contest. Even though this was her first bronc, she placed second. *From the private collection of Jack Davis, Olde America Antiques*

Mabel Strickland is shown in this postcard image with the title of World Champion Cowgirl.

As the darling of the rodeo circuit, she was often referred to by the press as well as the promoters as the "Lovely Lady of Rodeo." Another title bestowed upon this talented cowgirl was "Crown Princess of Rodeo" yet she was popular with her contemporary competitors being highly regarded and well liked by all.

Hugh Strickland died in 1941, Mabel re-married and settled near Buckeye, Arizona. She died in 1976. *Jack Davis Collection, Olde America Antiques*

MAYME SAUNDERS STROUD

A terrific Doubleday image on a photo postcard shows Mayme Stroud wearing a heavily fringed skirt waving her hat with a typical western hello.

This noted trick rider and bronc rider was married to Leonard Stroud inventor of the Stroud Stand Out, one of the most difficult of all trick riding maneuvers. Both Mayme and Leonard Stroud were avid fans of rodeo embracing the sport with unequaled passion. *Author's Collection*

A grand pose of Mayme Stroud riding *Black Bird* where she is wearing what appears to be a long corduroy double button skirt.

Mayme and Leonard called Rocky Ford, Colorado their home. On their letterhead and envelopes they had printed the statement: *If you can't catch him in five days, return to Leonard Stroud, World's Champion Trick Rider, Rocky Ford, Colorado.*

Mayme Stroud died April 1963. *From the private collection of Jack Davis, Olde America Antiques*

LORENA TRICKEY

A 1921 Doubleday image of Lorena Trickey lists her as Champion Cowgirl during the Frontier Days in Cheyenne, Wyoming.

This fierce competitor preferred the relay race and bucking contests. She is listed in the Bozeman Round Up for Friday August 6, 1920 for the Lady's Broncho Riding Contest riding *J.D. Watson*.

This controversial cowgirl was a proficient relay rider working for the C.B. Irwin relay strings. Very much a loner, she gained notoriety during a court trial for stabbing her cowboy lover to death. After being acquitted, Lorena attempted to capitalize on her unusual story, touring the country with an ill-fated stage act.

Fox Films Corporation employed Lorena Trickey to drive one of the racing chariots during the filming of Queen of Sheba, 1921.

The official souvenir program for 1925 Pendleton Round Up lists Lorena Trickey as competitor #45 for the Cowgirl's Relay Race for the Championship of the World, riding the Trickey String. One interesting side note to the program is the description of the winnings; $1100 to be divided $275.00 each day. Rules included 1 1/2 miles daily race with each rider to have three horses plus two assistants, one to hold and one to catch. Riders must touch ground with both feet in making horse changes; and will draw for place in paddock first day, thereafter in order in which they finish. Competitors for this day were Donna Cowan, Bonnie Gray, Helen Johnson and Lorena Trickey.

A past winner of the McAlpin trophy as World's Greatest Cowgirl, and winner of the Cowgirls Bronc Riding Championship, Lorena Trickey died in 1961. *From the private collection of Jack Davis, Olde America Antiques*

HAZEL WALKER

A tough ride is in store for Hazel Walker on *Buttons* during the Calgary Stampede. An entertaining note appears on the face of this postcard by Marcell, *"and she rode him."* It appears as though the snubber is afoot with the blindfold still on the bronc. Horse squeals abound! *Author's Collection*

VIVIAN WHITE

GRACE WHITE

GRACE WHITE TAKES BAD SPILL, ARK-OKLA RODEO (DOUBLEDAY)

Here is one of the most frightening sights for a rodeo spectator, cowgirl Grace White at the Arkansas-Oklahoma Rodeo takes a very "bad spill." Her sister Vivian White, an accomplished bronc rider herself, can be seen in this Doubleday photo, to the right of the chutes with her arm outstretched in an effort to help. *Credit: Wyoming State Museum*

The bronc *White Cloud* gives Vivian White a wonderful ride in this Stryker image from his famous "Photogloss" rodeo pictures series. This is a typical image for Stryker where he is looking up at the bronc giving the feeling of flight. *Author's Collection*

Stryker has captured Vivian White, Champion Cowgirl and Grace White's sister as she performs in the Grand Entry. Unfortunately this rodeo location is unknown, but based on the clothing, the date is possibly the early 1940s. This is one of Stryker's "Photogloss" images in his rodeo series 11. *Author's Collection*

One of the rarer images of an unknown cowgirl on her trick horse. Note her long, unborn calf split skirt. *Author's Collection*

In this photo the same cowgirl as in the previous photo shows her cowboy friend the buckle she probably won during a rodeo event. It is truly sad that their identities are unknown. *Author's Collection*

MAGGIE WRIGHT

Sadly Mrs. Ed (Maggie) Wright captured here by Doubleday just after she won the Lady Bronc contest in Cheyenne, Wyoming, 1917, was killed at Union Park in Denver, Colorado a few days after the image was taken. According to some accounts she was riding a bronc for a Hollywood movie when the horse fell backward over a fence. Maggie Wright's skull was fractured and she never regained consciousness. *Author's Collection* There also exists a rather unusual, larger image measuring 11x14 from the collection of John Fox, Montana. Larger postcard images are seldom found.

CHAPTER 2
GROUP PICTURES

Group shots, where the cowgirls are lined up at the rodeo site, or perhaps in a make-shift studio, seem to be the most desirable in collector terms. Value increases if the identity of the various cowgirls and the rodeo location are known. The earlier the date on the card, the better. The condition and resolution of the image on the postcard also factor into the value of the card.

Fashion evolution becomes rather obvious when reviewing these various group shots. Early on, the ladies wore the longer, heavy cloth skirts usually made of rugged corduroy. This length however, proved to be dangerous as the hems would often become caught in the saddle rigging prompting the more industrious ladies to use elastic bands below the knee which kept the skirt together. Lengths became shorter and with the use of the elastic, the bloomers were born followed closely by the jodhpurs. Pinning down the exact date when specific fashions were introduced is difficult as many cowgirls would wear their leather fringed skirts for show or parade, only to change later into their jodhpurs or pants for competition. Some of the ladies preferred the cloth skirts which they wore for the duration of their career. However, it is widely accepted that the majority of the ladies did prefer to wear pants by 1924 after having been introduced to them by Vera McGinnis

In her book *Rodeo Road* Vera McGinnis tells just how she came to wear pants. She was riding jumpers at the Ambassador Horse Show when she was inspired by a trick-riding act performed by Will Rogers' three children. "Mary Rogers wore long white-flannel pants exactly like her brothers'. They looked so neat and easy to work in compared with the tight breeches we wore, I thought, Why not?...The next week I had some made." Vera wore her new pants for the first time during the Fort Worth Fat Stock Show and according to the cowgirl they were a hit. During her 1924 trip to Europe with Tex Austin's show she had her complete new wardrobe fashioned with long pants. "When I returned to the states I found that many of the girls had followed my lead. Long pants were definitely in."

Blouses were generally loose fitting, made of very colorful silk or satin. Because many of the ladies had long hair, the use of large vivid hair bows was practically a requirement in order to keep their hair out of their face during an event. Styles of boots and hats for ladies followed the same general pattern as that for the men.

In terms of fashion, the flashier the better. Listed in the official souvenir program for the 1925 Pendleton Round Up is a cash prize of $5.00 given to the most typical cowboy and cowgirl in the Grand Mounted March. One cowgirl referred to this wardrobe display as "westerned up in their loud rags".

Taken at the Pendleton Round Up this Doubleday postcard captures the feeling of camaraderie and friendship that these women enjoyed. Even though most were fierce competitors they were also very close friends.

Pictured L to R is Kitty Canutt, Prairie Rose Henderson and Ruth Roach. Their outfits show the cross over from the corduroy split riding skirt Kitty wears to the always flashy embroidered clothing of Prairie Rose to the bloomers Ruth Roach wears. Both Kitty and Prairie Rose wear their spurs buckled to the inside as most of the early rodeo performers often did making it easier to remove them when necessary. Note too Prairie Rose has a horse lead rope tied around her waist and a quirt on her right arm. *Wyoming State Museum*

A very early photo dated 1909 taken by W. Martin of the four greatest lady riders in the world. Probably veterans of the Wild West shows, these cowgirls are wearing the long corduroy split skirts for riding. These long skirts were later shortened at the rodeo, with the aid of elastic garters placed just below the knees making them appear to be bloomers.

The longer split skirts were deemed dangerous as one of the girls became 'hung up' with her skirt entangled in the saddle rigging. Fortunately she escaped serious injury. After this incident, the girls began to shorten the skirts evolving into bloomers, jodphurs and eventually 'drop front' type slacks to today's denim jeans. *Author's Collection*

True renegades were these rodeo types in their dress and manners even when not in public view. The London Daily Express reported on the continual happenings while the cowboys and cowgirls were aboard the S.S. Menominee en route to England for Tex Austin's 1924 *First International Rodeo or Cowboy Championships.*

..."Cowgirls' fashions would drive a dress designer to despair... the girls, who are all beautiful, wear weird and costly clothes. One appeared at lunch in a pink silk boudoir cap. Most cowgirls appear at breakfast wearing afternoon hats and sleeveless frocks. All wear immense diamond and platinum rings. The indulgent cowboy husbands, wearing rags themselves, insist on their wives appearing at all times in full finery. There is a strange contrast in the outfits of the husbands and wives. The cowgirls rouge to excess, while the husbands are unshaven. The *Menominee* is now an exact replica of a Wild West saloon or a floating ranch. The cowboys sprawl on the floor playing dice. The wives dance to the gramophone or piano.".

Most of the cowgirls were accomplished seamstresses often making not only their own clothes but ostentatious shirts for their cowboy husbands. Few manufacturers, with the possible exception of the fringed leather skirts, produced rodeo rags early on but sensing the need for such outfits, they soon began churning out what the Wild West performer wanted. Later these styles were accepted by the fans as they began wearing outlandish, colorful clothing themselves when attending the rodeos.

Posed group photos are high on the collector's list with those taken during the rodeo especially desirable.

This group photo of the Champion Cowgirls was taken by Doubleday at the Pendleton Round Up September 1918. Only a few of these ladies can be identified: fourth from the left, sitting on the fence is Prairie Rose Henderson; to her left is one of the only black cowgirls, known only as Mrs. Sherry; and crouched in front is Fox Hastings. Note the fine, fringed and tacked leather skirts worn by the two cowgirls on the left.

The reverse of this postcard provides the flavor of the Round Up stating...

"we arrived here (Pendleton) about half past 5 o'clock last night...it was warm and dusty on the trip...the train was not crowded at all...saw some of the Uniontown (Washington) kids...the band from Camp Lewis was playing this morning...25 to 30 men." *Author's Collection*

One of the more highly desirable postcards, this image was taken during Tucumcari Round Up, either 1916 or 1919. A rare image, it shows the skirt variations including the fringed leather types to the corduroy with the second girl from the left having used elastic arm bands to "bloomer" her corduroy skirt just below the knee. These cowgirls were merely termed "trick riders and broncho busters." *Author's Collection*

Taken during the 1919 Pendleton Round Up, this image by W.S. Bowman features first, second and third place winners listed from left to right: Eloise (Fox) Hastings, Third; Ruth Roach, Second; and Lorena Trickey, First. It is unknown exactly what event they had participated in; however, the shoes Lorena Trickey wears might suggest it was a relay race. *Author's Collection*

The reverse side of this postcard is postmarked January 1920. Taken by Foster Photo Company in Miles City, Montana, this card features three competing cowgirls with the lady in the center identified as Mildred Douglas. On the front of the card are the words "Cow Girls & Good Ones." Note both Mildred Douglas and the lady to her right hold quirts. *Author's Collection*

A Doubleday photo of the relay riders during the Cheyenne Frontier Days pre 1920. L to R Mrs. Sherry, Montana Bell and Mayme Stroud. Because they are relay riders, their clothing for the contest was not flashy as they had to be ready for speed during the race. This is one of the few cards which identified the black cowgirl as Mrs. Sherry.

On the reverse of this card is the following;

> "..three cowgirls which were in some of the fast races. They can ride a poney (sic) some. I saw them ride five different races. We all yelled 'Stay with her horse' as they would pass by us. One mile track. I don't know who the soldier boy is in the picture...."

Due to that soldier boy's uniform the date can be established as 1920 or before. *Author's Collection*

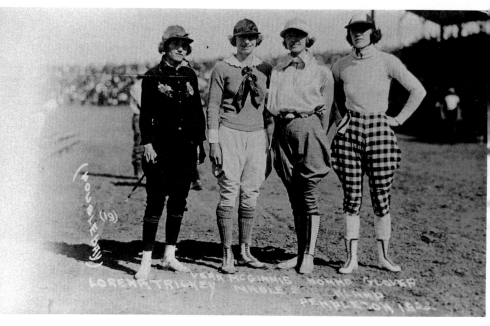

In a 1922 image, Doubleday has recorded the winners of the Pendleton Round Up relay race: L to R Lorena Trickey, Vera McGinnis, Mabel Strickland and Donna Glover. Note that jodphurs and jockey caps were the outfit of the day. *From the private collection of Jack Davis, Olde America Antiques*

By 1924 the Rodeo Cowgirls were in their heyday. This Doubleday image taken in Cheyenne, Wyoming shows the leading cowgirls posing in front of a group of Plains Indians. L to R Ruth Roach, Florence Hughes Randolph, Bea Kirnan, Bonnie Gray, Rose Smith, Toots Griffith and Ruby Roberts.

No doubt their dress was very flashy with the large silk scarves, colorful waist sashes and lively stitched boots. *Author's Collection*

Here is the reverse side of the previous postcard. Note the postmark is dated July 24, 1924 with a message letting the folks back home know "...I was here. They sure had some doing here. The biggest crowd. Cheyenne just flowed over with people, am going back tonite..." *Author's Collection*

Taken probably in the early thirties, this postcard by Doubleday shows, L to R Donna Card (Glover), Lorena Tricky and Mabel Strickland with some Indians posing at the Cheyenne Frontier Days. Lorena Tricky must have had a bad fall, note her left arm is in a sling. *Author's Collection*

An interesting assortment of ladies at the rodeo taken by Doubleday as they sit atop the fence. Doubleday has captioned the photo "Cow girls from the western ranches." While their identities are unknown perhaps the "Barn No. 1" behind them could give a clue to the location, probably taken in the mid 20s. Note the very colorful satin shirts, scarves and beautifully patterned boots. *Author's Collection*

This scene shows seven top cowgirl performers during the Triangle Ranch Rodeo as photographed by Doubleday.

Pictured L to R is Ruth Roach, Florence Hughes, Mabel Strickland, Bonnie Gray, Fox Hastings, Bea Kirnan and Toots Griffith. Judging from the assembled ladies, it could be determined that these were the winners in their various categories during this rodeo.

Several shots were taken at this same time of which this is one example. *Wyoming State Museum*

Another pose of the same cowgirls shown in the previous picture, taken at the same location, also by Doubleday. This one has the girls with their hats removed and the photographer has added an eighth cowgirl. Another photo taken at this same time adds the winning cowboys from the Triangle Ranch Rodeo to the group. (Not shown in this book) *Author's Collection*

Having your picture taken with a performing animal seemed to be the activity of the day. Even though we do not know the location, the cowgirls are L to R Prairie Rose, Vera McGinnis, Donna Glover, Mabel Strickland and Bonnie McCarroll. Judging from the clothing, this could have been taken around 1930. A Doubleday postcard. *Author's Collection*

This Doubleday photo again shows the different fashions the cowgirls chose to wear. L to R Reine Hafley, Fox Hastings, Rose Smith, Ruth Roach, Mabel Strickland, Prairie Rose and Dorothy Morrell. Note Dorothy Morrell's contestant ribbon plus the words "Champion woman rider" written over Mabel Strickland. *Author's Collection*

Taken probably around 1930, this Doubleday image features the top competitors and performers from a particular rodeo. L to R is Rose Smith, Donna Glover, Bonnie McCarroll, Mabel Strickland and Fox Hastings.

Rose Smith holds her trick riding shoes and is wearing what might be a Pendleton Round Up scarf. Both Donna Glover and Bonnie McCarroll have their contestant numbers on their right hips and all five cowgirls are wearing what appear to be very colorful rodeo togs. *Wyoming State Museum*

DONNA GLOVER   MABLE STRICKLAND
ROSE SMITH   BONNIE McCARROLL FOX HASTINGS

The Los Angeles Rodeo produced a fine turnout of cowgirls including those in this Doubleday postcard. Note all the various clothing and hat styles which seem to cross over the different time frames. This appears to be from the mid 1920s.

It is worth noting their love of large hats, colorful scarves and fancy dress throughout the years the ladies performed and competed in rodeo. *From the private collection of Jack Davis, Olde America Antiques*

COWGIRLS AT THE LOS ANGELES ROUND-UP
(DOUBLEDAY)

In practically the same image as the previous one, here is another postcard of the Los Angeles Rodeo cowgirls but with a few changes, the girls have removed their hats! Doubleday must have asked them to do so as this is not the first series of images in which hats are on then off. *Author's Collection*

COWGIRLS AT THE LOS ANGELES ROUND-UP

Taken during the 1925 Pendleton Round Up by Doubleday, here is a group of 6 contest winners. Rose Smith is the one on the far left. *From the private collection of Jack Smith, Olde America Antiques*

The Tex Austin Rodeo in Chicago had many cowgirls as is shown in the Doubleday postcard. Note the contestant numbers on the girl's arms. The three ladies on the far right are Fox Hastings, Toots Griffith and Ruth Roach.

Note the cowgirl fourth from the left. This is one of the first examples of fancy colored leather inlaid boots.

From the private collection of Jack Davis, Olde America Antiques

The relay race winners are shown in this 1928 Pendleton Round Up Doubleday postcard. L to R Mabel Strickland, Vera McGinnis, Donna Cowan and Josephine Wicks. *From the private collection of Jack Davis, Olde America Antiques*

Taken in 1930 at the Houston Show by Doubleday this is one of the more highly collectible images as it contains some of the most popular and successful cowgirl rodeo participants. L to R Bea Kirnan, Rose Smith, Mabel Strickland, Fox Hastings, Ruth Roach, and Florence Hughes Randolph. This particular scene shows the studio shot which was later cropped to create one of Doubleday's postcards.

There were several individual photos taken of these cowgirls during the same session which probably lasted most of the day. In addition to the standing pose shown above, Doubleday also photographed the girls in a group scene with some standing and some sitting, then each girl individually standing, sitting and on her horse. *Wyoming State Museum*

This 1921 publicity photo by Doubleday features five lady trick riders in the Hippodrome pose. Because their names are not indicated on the postcard identity of these talented performers is difficult; however, the third from the left is one of the few black cowgirls, Mrs. Sherry. *Wyoming State Museum*

Photographers seemed to focus on the individual when he or she performed in the arena making these parade images and cowgirl race scenes very rare. Because the rodeo fan often preferred to purchase a card of the winning competitor rather than just a generic rodeo scene, these cards were not in vogue at the time. Today, however, they are enjoying a new popularity due to their scarcity.

There were two rodeos that Will Stecker photographed, both were held in Gilman, Montana. While their titles are confusing, one was believed to be called the Gilman Stampede held in September 1919 and the second was called the Lewis and Clark Country Stampede held in 1920. Still, the names of these two rodeos tended to become one. Nevertheless, only about 14 photos of these two rodeos exist most of which are included in this collection. They are extremely rare not only for their historical significance, but for the fact that these are probably the only rodeo images taken by Stecker.

"Cow Girls" at the PENDLETON "ROUND UP" 1911

This is a close up view of the famous Marcell photo taken during the Pendleton Round Up. Note the center cowgirl holding a sign which reads "Queen of the Round Up." *Author's Collection*

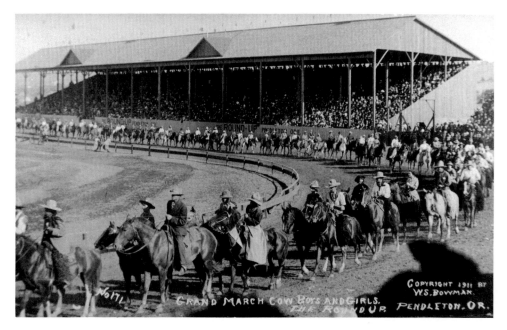

Another image of the Grand March, this taken by W.S. Bowman in 1911 during the Pendleton Round Up. This early scene clearly shows the size of this most popular rodeo. Note the very long skirt worn by one of the ladies in the foreground. *Author's Collection*

"Cowboy's and Cowgirls Grand March."
PHOTO, BY ROUND-UP ASS'N.
51
PENDLETON, ORE., 1921

A splendid view of the grand march, again from Pendleton, Oregon in 1921. Note the two cowgirls just behind the lead Appaloosa horse. One of the ladies wears long jodhpurs while the other wears what appears to be a leather fringe skirt outfit. *Author's Collection*

In this 1922 Doubleday photo taken at the popular Pendleton Round Up is Thelma Thompson Queen of the Round Up. Four mounted ladies are just behind her, they might be her royal court. Note the queen's lovely fringe skirt and fancy jacket. *From the private collection of Jack Davis, Olde America Antiques*

THELMA THOMPSON QUEEN OF THE ROUND-UP, 1922
DOUBLEDAY (C)
PENDLETON, OREGON.

The Cowgirls' Race at Frontier.
Frontier Days, Cheyenne, Wyoming. Aug. 20-21-22.

In a rare action packed image, these cowgirls race during the Frontier Days in Cheyenne, Wyoming August 1922. This image could be either from the flat race or from a portion of the relay races. *Author's Collection*

63

"THEY'RE OFF" COW GIRLS RACE.
CHEYENNE FRONTIER DAYS - 1932.

OUT WEST PHOTO SERVICE DENVER.

The Out West Photo Service from Denver, Colorado had one of its photographers capture the beginning of the cowgirl's race at the Cheyenne Frontier Days in 1932. Note the ladies' use of long pants and jockey type hats rather than their usual 'Stetsons'. *Author's Collection*

This W.S. Bowman photo was taken during the Pendleton Round Up possibly in 1911 due to the clearly visible long skirts. The notes written at the top of the image state..."the most thrilling and exciting race of the round up" indicates the love the fans held for the cowgirl's races. *Author's Collection*

No 381 W.S.BOWMAN HOTO COWGIRLS PONY RACE. ROUND UP.

W.S.BOWMAN PHOTO No 67. COWGIRL'S PONY RACE. THE ROUND UP PENDLETON O.

Another view taken during the Pendleton Round Up shows a race which Ella Lazinka (Lozinka some sources list) won. Note again the handwriting, the same that appears on the face of previous card..."this was taken the first day when Ella Lazinka won. Her horse is shown in the lead." Cowgirl races were held daily during the round up and this is a different race from that in the preceding image, yet it was taken during the same round up. Ella once competed against famed cowgirl Bertha Blancett, defeating her in 1911 and 1912. Well on her way to becoming a top racing cowgirl, an injury in 1915 prevented Ella Lazinka from further competition. *Author's Collection*

During the Tex Austin's 1922 Rodeo in Chicago, a photographer captured a rare scene of a cowgirl changing horses in mid air during a relay race. Soon after this, the competition rules were modified to insist the cowgirl must touch the ground between mounts.

The ladies relay race, one of the most popular, exciting round up events for the early cowgirl began in 1898 and lasted through 1946. In the very beginning days of rodeo, the show consisted mostly of races for both men and women, plus a pitching and bucking contest and a couple of shows with the stagecoach and possibly a brass band. Cheyenne Frontier Days claimed 1906 as the beginning of the ladies relay race.

Typically the cowgirls would be hired by the owner of the string of horses. When the cowgirl would win, the purse would generally be divided between her and the owner of the string, depending on her contractual agreements. For the Frontier Days held annually in Cheyenne, Wyoming, the prize money was the largest purse of any of the women's events. In addition, the winner was awarded a large silver loving cup which was donated by the sponsor of the race, The Denver Post.

For the relay race itself, each rider used three horses completing a 1 1/2 mile race track changing horses after 1/2 a mile. In the early days, the cowgirls used only one saddle having to unsaddle, re-saddle and re-mount each horse without help from the assistant. Due to haste in re-saddling the horse during the contest, mistakes were made and accidents happened, thus the rules were changed to allow for all three

A FAST CHANGE
COWGIRLS RELAY RACE.
TEX AUSTIN'S RODEO - CHICAGO

horses to be saddled and the rider merely had to 'fly' from one horse to another. However, this too became dangerous as the highly competitive cowgirls literally threw caution to the wind in changing horses, so the practice of leaping through the air from horse to horse was quickly abandoned. *Author's Collection*

During the first week of September in 1919 and 1920 a rodeo was held in Gilman, Montana which was photographed by Will Stecker. Even though he was a well established and talented photographer in his day, this is probably the only rodeo he captured on film.

First in this extremely rare series, is a very crudely assembled lead-in postcard. It appears as though he simply tore images out of the photos and pasted them together, then photographed that assemblage, placing the title of the rodeo in the center heart. The date indicated on this is September 2,3,4 of 1919 yet there are images included in the montage which are from the 1920 Lewis & Clark County Stampede, also called the Gilman Stampede. Apparently the two titles were interchangeable.

All Gilman rodeo Will Stecker images are from the private collection of Jack Davis, Olde America Antiques

Unidentified cowgirls race during the 1920 Gilman Stampede.

Mrs. Rose Smith rides a wild steer for the Gilman 1919 stampede.

Miss Williams has just changed horses during the relay race for the Gilman Stampede, 1919.

John Dozier presents Tex Smith with his prize, a hand tooled saddle for winning the Lewis & Clark Stampede in Gilman, Montana. Note Mrs. Smith's long corduroy split riding skirt and bolero type vest.

Mrs. Tex Smith participated in the Lewis & Clark County Stampede as evidenced by this photo of her trick riding.

Another view of Mrs. Tex Smith performing her trick riding during the Lewis & Clark County Stampede, Gilman, Montana.

In addition to trick riding, Mrs. Tex Smith also competed in the bucking horse contest as seen in this photo of her riding "the buckskin horse" during the Lewis & Clark County Stampede.

Mr. & Mrs. Tex Smith walk across the arena after Tex's ride on a bronc during the Lewis & Clark County Stampede.

Another view of Mrs. Tex Smith on a bronc called *The Blue Horse* during the Lewis & Clark County Stampede.

Mrs. Hall is seen here taking a bad fall during the 1920 Gilman Stampede.

This is an extremely rare photo of Fannie Sperry Steele on a wild steer during the Gilman Stampede in 1920.

Another very rare photo postcard of Fannie Sperry Steele avoiding a collision with the bronc *Cheyenne*, taken during the Gilman Stampede in 1919.

CHAPTER 4
THE ROMANTIC IMAGES OF THE COWGIRL: PERFORMERS, ART CARDS AND ADVERTISING

Advertising in and of itself, is a very collectible category. Narrow it down to images of the Old West and the cowgirl emerges as a highly utopian figure gracing everything from calendars to coffee cans. Firearms and ammunition were often sold by beautiful images of the American cowgirl. Items which feature these delightful yet alluring cowgirls are most desirable to the collector with rather high values due primarily to their scarcity.

Art cards are postcard images of the cowgirl painted by contemporary artists most of whom were professional illustrators of their day and did not specialize in any particular subject. They romanticized their "women of the west" subjects as many artists appeared to have unrealistic fantasies about the true cowgirl. These cards were, for the most part, printed in color adding to their collectibility. There is an entire area for what is known as silk cards which generally came on the scene in the 1950's. Some are included here. Values for these art card postcards depend on the clarity of image, color reproduction, art style and the artist himself.

Occasionally a photographer would capture an image involving cowgirls for the sole purpose of a story or comic type postcard. One series of these actual photo art cards of a cowboy wooing his cowgirl, is included in this collection.

Taking the cowgirl from the Western prairie to the East coast theater thereby romancing her image, was done with reckless abandon. Numerous lady performers would don the rags of the western cowgirl and fabricate, on stage what they thought were the actions of these daring ladies of the West. As with the larger than life figures of Buffalo Bill and Ned Buntline whose heroic reputations and deeds of bravery were fictionalized, so too were the exploits of the cowgirls. Included in this collection are several images of these lady performers.

Just as those ladies on stage acted out their plays, so too did the ladies from the Wild West Exhibitions portray the wild and wooly cowgirl to a multitude of fans. Even though the context of this book deals primarily with the rodeo cowgirl, no book on the ladies who worked in the western arena would be complete without some images from cowgirls who performed with the Wild West shows. As indicated in previous chapters, many of these women would begin their careers with these Wild West shows gravitating eventually to the rodeo circuit. Many times, however, the cowgirls would perform in both professions in an effort to earn as much of a paycheck as they could.

A very unusual image in this photo art card depicts a lady dressed like a cowgirl atop a fake horse. Note the very interesting saddle that has military style pommel holsters, studded skirt and hooded stirrups. Around her waist is a rather large gunbelt and holster with pistol. Printed in Germany, the reverse side has the word for 'postcard' printed in 10 different languages including Russian. *Author's Collection*

The second unusual photo art card, also printed in Germany shows the same cowgirl atop a different fake horse. Here she is animated in a femme fatale pose. *Author's Collection*

Shy Ann, Shy Ann, hop on my pony.   Copyright 1907. De Witt C. Wheeler.

A delightful series of four story photo art cards presents the development of a romance, printed by Theodor Eismann in Leipzig, Germany, and New York, copyrighted in 1907 by De Witt C. Wheeler. In the first image the original sender added an "A" at the end of the name Ann as apparently his intended was named Anna. Following a song popular at the time, *Shy Ann, Shy Ann* this card begins the tender story. "Shy Ann, Shy Ann, hop on my pony." Note the interested look on the horse's face! *Author's Collection*

In the next photo art card, the cowboy is helping his sweetheart onto his horse. Note that she is attempting to mount the horse from the 'off' or wrong side which apparently makes no difference to the horse. "There's room here, for two dear, but after the ceremony." *Author's Collection*

The third image celebrates the marriage of the two with their fellow cowboys shooting their pistols in revelry. Again, the horse seems to be interested in the activities. "On my pony, from old Cheyenne." *Author's Collection*

Finally, the two lovebirds honeymoon at their campsite while the horse now is totally indifferent to the whole scenario. "We'll both ride back home dear, as one,." *Author's Collection*

Hands Up   No. 104.   Copyrighted 1908. By S.D. Burcher & Son Kearney, Nebr.

This is a very unusual but early photo taken by S.D. Burcher & Son of Kearney, Nebraska and appears to be of a person who dressed up as a cowgirl just to have her photo made, a rather common practice. Note the chintz feel of the cloth, the bordered scarf and the seemingly early military type leggings worn over the shoes. Just for effect she appears to be taking aim with a small period pistol, hence the title "Hands Up." It is a nice horsy touch with her holding the quirt in her gloved hand. *Author's Collection*

COPYRIGHT 11-30-08 BY LILLIAN BELL OMAHA NEB. THE GIRL OF THE GOLDEN WEST.

A beautiful photo of a performing Wild West Cowgirl wearing an extremely fancy outfit with a copyright notice from Lillian Bell dated 1908. Titled "The Girl of the Golden West," she no doubt portrayed that fantasy image in the show. The design on her vest and gauntlets appears to be embroidery with the fringe sewn onto the skirt and vest. On her peaked hat she wears a pin of Indian design denoting the four winds. Oftentimes, ladies who did little or no horse work, wore street shoes which were covered by leggings clearly seen in this image. Because she holds a rope, she could have performed various rope tricks, or it could simply be a prop. *Author's Collection*

Here is an example of either a cowgirl posing for her picture in a studio setting, or it could be a lady who wanted to be dressed like a cowgirl performer for her picture. Note the chintz appearance of the cloth outfit, and she is holding a small pistol in her right hand. *From the private collection of Jack Davis, Olde America Antiques*

Occasionally the names are listed on the reverse side of photos; here is Laura Gayriell complete with a notation of "from Follies Show" which tells us this lady was most certainly an early performer. An autographed picture is desirable even though neither the lady nor her career is well known. Note her cloth fringed pants with tall leggings over beaded moccasins. She wears a very long bandanna and cloth hat.

Whenever a gun of any kind can be seen in the image, it increases the value of the photo. Certainly a publicity photo, this performer holds her nickel plated pistol as if she were taking aim. Including cardboard border, this photo measures 9" X 7" overall. *Author's Collection*

An actress assumes a decidedly adorable pose in this image taken by a New York Studio. Upon close examination the gun appears to be a stage prop, probably carved out of wood, and in her right arm she cradles a horse quirt. A cute image of Frankie Kimball, an early day stage performer in a cabinet photo measuring 6 1/2" tall by 4" wide. *Author's Collection*

Playing cards appeared to be important during the earlier part of this century for here this actress holds them in her hand as a prop. A publicity photo for either this young actress or for a stage play in which she appeared, this image clearly displays a rare, fully beaded Plains Indian style pipe bag suspended from her gunbelt. Her rifle is leaning against the table, another indication of her involvement in a western type stage act. This cabinet photo measures 6 1/2" X 4 1/4" wide. *Author's Collection*

→✳ ULLIE AKERSTROM. ✳←

FRANK WENDT, Photo. Artist   NEW YORK

This is a classic example of a performer dressing in the cowgirl's rags. Edith "Billy" Storey performed with the Vitagraph Players wearing a conversion split skirt, one which could be buttoned on either side to become a street skirt, or an actual split riding skirt. She also has the studded leather cuffs, spur straps and matching belt, a colorful scarf, period hat and hand tooled boots. An adorable image full of playful spirit, probably from the early 1900s. *From the private collection of Jack Davis, Olde America Antiques*

Thecla Hunting was an English actress who appears here in full cowgirl type costume. Her cuffs appear to be made of cloth yet her skirt seems to be leather. On her hip is a pistol in a leather holster, making this a desirable image. *From the private collection of Jack Davis, Olde America Antiques*

Another guessing game, is this lady a performer or is she yet another who simply wished to have her photo taken wearing western garb? A very colorful rodeo scarf, worn beaded gauntlets and a holster which is way too big for the pistol housed in it, create the appearance of a "western lady." Unfortunately, the reasons behind this image are lost to father time. *From the private collection of Jack Davis, Olde America Antiques*

This 1908 pose of Annie Schafer clearly shows her 4 3/4" barrel, smokeless powder Colt Single Action tucked in her belt. One of the few ladies in this series of performers who is wearing boots complete with spurs. She also wears a long, split riding skirt and full sleeved blouse. An additional photo of Annie Schafer, found in the Buffalo Bill Museum, shows her kneeling down pulling a rope. These were apparently some publicity photos taken to promote her and a Wild West Show. Not mounted onto a cabinet card, this original photo measures 5 3/4" tall by 4" wide. *Author's Collection*

During the Wild West era, from about 1890 through 1920s, there were many Annie Oakley type, crack shot ladies who would perform with the various traveling shows and circuses. Here is an interesting view of a typical performing lady wearing her fully fringed cloth outfit, long strands of beads and a cape. Again, this lady wears no boots but prefers leggings over street shoes. Note the contrasting trimmed hat complete with stars sewn onto the brim. She holds what is probably her favorite rifle. The dog is stuffed in this 6 1/2" tall by 4 1/4" wide, gold-edged cabinet photo. *Author's Collection*

On the reverse side of this period photo is the caption, "Lone Star May, the great woman shot, in action." Unfortunately, the photographer did not take this image so that her face can be seen to confirm her identity possibly as May Lillie. Here is another example of the many crack shot performing women from the Wild West era.

Note the stars on the edge of her turned up hat which was an effect copied from the famous Annie Oakley. Her dress appears to be made of velvet with sewn on fringe; she wears street shoes over which can be seen heavily buckled leggings. This photo measures the typical 6 3/4" by 4 3/4" wide, ready for mounting onto a card. *Author's Collection*

Perhaps the best known lady performer from the Wild West era is Annie Oakley, or "Little Sure Shot" as nicknamed by the Ogallala Sioux Chief Sitting Bull. This is an image from a "CDV" or Carte de Visite which is a small calling card bearing the person's image on one side, and name on the reverse. This CDV measures 4" tall by 2 1/2" wide.

This CDV is a beautiful pose of Annie Oakley dressed in a lovely embroidered outfit, holding her Stevens .22 calibre rifle and standing next to a velvet drape onto which is pinned her various competition badges from shooting matches. Note the familiar star sewn onto the brim of her hat. While never a true cowgirl by definition, Annie Oakley is often the name that is mentioned when the subject of cowgirls is broached. *Author's Collection*

Here is a rare Eisenmann 6 1/2" X 4 1/4" cabinet photo of Annie Oakley from a New York Studio. A second photo of Annie posing with Texas Ben was also taken at this time, but not included here. Photographed early in her career, Annie wears a tan cotton dress decorated with appliques, sewn on fringe and woodland Indian beaded moccasins. Note the absence of the star on her hat brim, a feature she adopted later in her career. Around her waist she wears a gunbelt complete with holster and a pistol with pearl grips. A lovely, very scarce item complete with gold edging on the card. *Author's Collection*

Over the course of Wild West collecting, perhaps the most famous photos found are those taken of this delightful young woman who posed for George Cornish from Arkansas City, Kansas. The three images shown here were all taken in 1909 and stated that this lovely lady worked with the 101 Ranch. Each photo has a different title printed on its face and measures 7 3/4" tall by 6" wide.

The first in this series is "The Belle of the Ranch" where she is seen with her stuffed horse (look at his eye) who dons a magnificent leather studded bridle while the cowgirl wears a larger than life gunbelt and holster complete with a Colt Bisley. *Author's Collection*

The last in the series is an intriguing view of the cowgirl wearing a buckskin shirt and pointing a gun directly at the camera. Her belt and holster set, which are too large for her, bears the brand name "Olive." *Author's Collection*

The second in this series shows a somber cowgirl in the image titled "The Flower of the Prairie" with her hands neatly settled onto a large rope. Note the lovely Navajo style silver button on her hat. *Author's Collection*

Many ladies performed with the Miller's Brother's 101 Ranch shows, often leaving for a time to work the rodeo circuit in an effort to earn as much money as possible. This unusual photo postcard is of twin cowgirl performers, the Parry sisters, taken by the photographer Floyd. *From the private collection of Jack Davis, Olde America Antiques*

As a companion image to the previous one, here are the Parry sisters performing on their matching mounts for the Miller's Brothers 101 Ranch Wild West Show. *From the private collection of Jack Davis, Olde America Antiques*

PARRY SISTERS (Twins), 101 Ranch Cow Girls

Many of the cowgirls not only performed with the various Wild West shows, but also with the various circus groups. Probably taken in the late 1920s, judging from the automobile in the background, is a performing cowgirl rearing her horse. She is riding a sidesaddle, which is possibly why she looks awkward in the seat. *Author's Collection*

From the 101 ranch is Verna Schultz posing here in this photo postcard, on her horse in front of the Indian Encampment. Verna is wearing a beautiful, multi layered fringed skirt and hat typical for the period. Note her performer ribbon pinned to her shirt.

Quoting from the 101 Ranch publication called the Advance Courier, an illustrated periodical published by Miller Brothers and Edward Arlington's 101 Ranch, Wild West season of 1910 is this delightful definition of the western cowgirl as she relates to the Wild West show:

"Among the horses, steers, broncos, buffaloes, cowboys, Indians and other concomitants of the 'wild and woolly' west which the famous 101 ranch is bringing to this city is an element new to this community - the cowgirl. The cowgirl is a development of the stock-raising West comparing with the bachelor girl and the independent woman of the East. She is not of the new woman class -- not of the sort that discards her feminine attributes and tries to ape the man, simply a lively, athletic young woman with a superfluity of nerve and animal spirits with a realization that in affairs where skill is the chief qualification she has an equal chance with her brothers."
Author's Collection

The Miller's Brothers 101 Ranch Wild West Show featured many cowgirls performing various acts, and this area of collecting offers a multitude of levels for the collector including artifacts, photos, histories of the various specific personalities and the like. Here is a terrific postcard image of a performing ranch cowgirl wearing fully beaded gauntlets, a colorful satin blouse and wide brimmed hat. Her horse is decked out in a beautiful studded leather bridle. *Author's Collection*

During the early 1900s several traveling Wild West shows performed for the British at various locations. The Red Man Spectacle was performed at Earls Court a working arena located in the Knight's Bridge district of London where several cowgirls performed with the group. In this photo taken in England, Lucille Pease wears a very unbecoming outfit: Her gun belt and pistol are slung far too low and the clothes do not appear to fit. The beauty of this card however, is the fact that she did sign it "Lucille Pease, Texas Cowgirl," adding to its value. *Author's Collection*

Lillian Bergerhoff is (sic) one of the ladies from the Red Man Spectacle held in Earls Court. Apparently, the photographer had difficulty correctly spelling the ladies' names for the printed name on the face of the postcard differs from her autograph. Her actual name was Lillian Berghofer and she hailed from Cheyenne, Wyoming.

Sadly the Red Man Spectacle was interrupted by the outbreak of WWI. All their gear, equipment and livestock were confiscated leaving the performers to find their own way home to the United States. *From the private collection of Jack Davis, Olde America Antiques*

Lillian Bergerhoff.
A Cow Girl taking part in the Red Man Spectacle, Earls Court.

This is the first in a series of four portrait cards again taken during The Red Man Spectacle in Earls Court. Here Ada Brayfield, Champion Lady Revolver Shot of South Dakota poses with her 5 1/2," smokeless powder, Colt Single Action. Each lady autographed these postcards with her name and home town; Ada Brayfield was from Denver Colorado. *From the private collection of Jack Davis, Olde America Antiques*

In a wistful pose, Lillian Bergerhoff (sic), Champion Lady Rope Twirler of Texas, is one of the cowgirls who performed with the Red Man Spectacle in Earls Court. Again, this card is signed by the cowgirl, Lillian Berghofer from Cheyenne, Wyoming. Note the ribbons she has tied just above her elbow to hold up the billowy sleeves on the blouse. All the photos from this series were taken by Cale and Polden & Co. and printed on postcards in England. *From the private collection of Jack Davis, Olde America Antiques*

Continuing the Earls Court series, this is of Lucille Pease with the title of Champion Wild Steer Rider of Wyoming. She autographed the card with her name, and hometown of Angleton, Texas. It appears as though each lady wears the same holster and belt set and holds the same gun in each image. *From the private collection of Jack Davis, Olde America Antiques*

In a rather coy pose is Jane Bermondy (sic), Champion Relay Rider of Colorado. This autographed card of Jane Bernoudy who hailed from Douglas, Arizona continues the Earls Court series. Note her beaded arm bands, leather cuffs and the same basket weave leather holster all the other ladies wore. She points the gun directly at the camera just over her elbow.

Jane Bernoudy was often referred to as the first cowgirl trick roper and traveled with the C.B. Irwin Wild West Show. Like many of her sisters, Jane Bernoudy went to Hollywood where she did some bit parts and was once engaged to the western movie star William S. Hart. *From the private collection of Jack Davis, Olde America Antiques*

Peterson completed a series of cowgirl/out west illustrations includin[g] this one entitled "Corralled," another idealistic interpretation of th[e] cowgirl and her cowboy. Note the tiny illustration in the lower rig[ht] hand corner of a cowgirl holding a rather large gun. Published by H.[H.] Tammen, Denver, copyrighted in 1906. *Author's Collection*

Dated 1908, this full color art card by Peterson features "The Queen [o]f the Bar Tee Ranch" a stylized, enticing cowgirl complete with her [h]olster in the cross-draw position. This was copyrighted by H.H. [T]ammen of Denver, Colorado. *Author's Collection*

One of two images included in this collection, entitled the "Troilene western types series" painted by John Innes. This is the "Cattle Girl" color art card published by W.G. Macfarlane, New York, Buffalo and Toronto, 1908. On the reverse is the following description:
"CATTLE GIRL. Born on the ranch, accustomed all her life to the freedom of the range, the Cattle Girl is not content to assume the duties of a house too early in life, and she may be frequently met cruising for cattle or visiting outlying camps. Her ideas are usually as wide as are the great reaches over which she rides, and as clean as the mountain-born stream she fords."
Clearly a utopian attitude towards the concept of the cowgirl. *From the private collection of Jack Davis, Olde America Antiques*

Another in the "Troilene western types series" painted by John Innes is "The Bronco Girl." Reverse side of this art card imparts the following information: "The Bronco Girl. It is inevitable that a girl bred and reared amongst the strenuous life of cow-men and bronco-busters, should contract those habits of fearlessness and ambition to conquer the brute world so characteristic of all dwellers on the ranches. Thus occurred the 'Bronco Girl'. She can ride, she can shoot, and when time has toned her down, she makes the ideal rancher's wife." Copyrighted 1908, this description provides some insight into what was a socially acceptable attitude during that era for the western cowgirl. *Author's Collection*

One of four illustrations included here in another series of color art cards show stylized interpretations of the cowgirls. This card was published in 1910 and is titled "A Daughter of the West" shown in the act of roping. *Author's Collection*

Another in the series created by the same artist, shows this cowgirl wearing fringed leggings, on her horse taking aim from the left-handed position. This color art card is embossed, with the cowgirl and her horse in full relief. Printed in Germany for the United Art Publishing Co of New York City. *Author's Collection*

The third in this series shows the cowgirl searching the horizon while atop her ready stead; her gun and holster appear to float on her skirt. This particular art card was printed in Germany for the S. Langsdorf & Co. in New York. *Author's Collection*

The final image in this series shows the cowgirl firing her pistol while another lady in the background throws a lasso. No printer or publisher is indicated on this fine embossed color art card. *Author's Collection*

Reynolds, another illustrator whose style can be easily detected, again romances the cowgirl in this series of three art cards. Here the image is titled "Hurry Up" as the cowgirl motions to the rest of the riders behind her. *From the private collection of Jack Davis, Olde America Antiques*

Reynolds continues his series of art cards with this image entitled "Rodeo" where the demure cowgirl ropes a steer. *From the private collection of Jack Davis, Olde America Antiques*

The final image in the Reynolds series depicts a cowgirl off her horse, searching the horizon and is entitled "A Long Way Home." *From the private collection of Jack Davis, Olde America Antiques*

In a more aggressive image, this cowgirl has her horse down and is taking aim against her foe with a Remington revolver. Note the English style riding boots in this art card copyrighted 1906 by J. Ellsworth Gross, entitled "Dead Shot," published by Williamson Haffner Co., Denver. *Author's Collection*

DEAD SHOT.

Another image by J. Ellsworth Gross shows the cowgirl again off her horse and is entitled "Watching the Round-Up." Published by Williamson Haffner Co. of Denver, copyrighted 1906. *Author's Collection*

A light, airy image of a western cowgirl complete with hat, riding quirt, gauntlets and low slung gun belt. *From the private collection of Jack Davis, Olde America Antiques*

This is a very interesting card not only for the illustration entitled "The Range Land Girl" by impressionist artist Gollings but for its early indications of international commercialism. Copyrighted 1908 by Range Land Publishing Company of Sheridan, Wyoming, this card was actually printed in Germany. *From the private collection of Jack Davis, Olde America Antiques*

An unusual photo art card which has been embellished with artistic rendering shows a cowgirl in a saloon with her pistol drawn. The story is unclear but the message for a loose life is "It all end's in smoke." *Author's Collection*

A wild buffalo hunt by a cowgirl is portrayed by artist F. V. Smith in this color art card. Apparently this was a series of cards as indicated by the logo "The Buffalo Hunt" in the lower right hand corner. The date on the postmark is 1916. *Author's Collection*

Here is a photo color-enhanced art card copyrighted 1908 by Charles E. Morris of Chinook, Montana. This particular image is from his "Cow Girl Series No. 2 - It looks like trouble - maybe it's Indians" which indicates the universal acceptance that in the early 1900s the threat of an Indian uprising still existed. *Author's Collection*

Entitled "A Cow Girl looking for the Herd" this photo, color enhanced art card was copyrighted in 1908 by Charles E. Morris Co. of Great Falls, Montana and he also published this card. Note her long skirt, short crown hat and leather gunbelt with a pearl handled pistol. This appears to be the same cowgirl and horse as seen in the previous image. *Author's Collection*

A series of three included in this collection of lovely cowgirl portraits that appear to be photographs enhanced with some painting of the image. These images are copyrighted 1912 by Schlesinger Brothers of New York, who also published them. *Author's Collection*

This is a very interesting color photo art card which has been enhanced by an artist. A "Cow Girl with Buffalo Bill's Wild West" is shown ready to draw her pistol and holding a bull whip, while at her feet is a horse-hair bridle. Note her full red scarf, small brimmed hat with beaded hat band and her white, woolly chaps. *Author's Collection*

A Daughter of the West

Another "Daughter of the West" by an unknown artist shows the typical cowgirl, armed and ready for action. *Author's Collection*

729. Cow-Girl.

Entitled "Cow-Girl" this image shows a coquettish yet confident cowgirl ready to draw her pistol. This particular image was used by many firms including the Williamson Haffner Co. of Denver, 1907. *Author's Collection*

Part of their "cowboys series" is this photo art card, color enhanced titled "Trying the lasso." *Author's Collection*

Another similar to the previous photo art card which has been color enhanced is entitled "Fun on the Ranch." Note the ladies typical cowgirl type clothing. *Author's Collection*

Shooting up the Town

When we've rounded up the cattle
   And the sun's gone down,
You would think there was a battle
   If you follered us to town;
For we're out for all that's comin'
And we keep the town a-hummin'
When we're rollickin' and frolickin'
   We do things brown.

Western Girl Series No. 7.   WALTER JUAN DAVIS

Artists of the period loved to give pistols to the ladies in their images even though the real cowgirls were rarely armed. In this cartoon image is a cowgirl drawn by Walter Juan Davis in his western girl series No. 7 shooting up the town after a cattle round up. This art card was published by The Thayer Publishing Co. in Denver, Colorado, and is postmarked 1909. *Author's Collection*

Printed in Germany, this art card of an idealized cowgirl rides her rearing mount while shooting her pistol in a valentine titled "My Hearty Greeting." *Author's Collection*

NOW LOOK WHOSE HERE
She's a nifty little cowboy girl
    as cute as can be found
And she's known by everybody
    on the range for miles aroud
But she doesn't need a chaperon
    to make the boys be nice
She has a big six shooter
    which she knows will quite suffice

Created by Sanglier in 1908, this stylized image of the cowgirl includes another reference to a pistol. Apparently these ladies of the West were armed and dangerous! *Author's Collection*

I like to spoon with my pal

A really cute image of a cowboy and a cowgirl sharing lunch with the title "I like to spoon with my pal" implying a romantic scenario. Art cards such as these were often sent between lovers as is evidenced by the reverse side which contains a love poem, dated 1913. *Author's Collection*

C.T. Dude Ranch Comics published a series of 10 subjects in art card form of which this is one, depicting a dude cowgirl on her galloping horse. On the reverse it states this art postcard to be "genuine curteich-Chicago 'C.T. Art-colortone' post card." Note the Anglo Indian by the tipi with the "for rent" sign. *From the private collection of Jack Davis, Olde America Antiques*

Another image in the C.T. Dude Ranch comics series is this one of a cowgirl waiting for her horse to be saddled. In collecting these types of art cards, it is a wise choice to attempt to gather the entire set of 10 which would make the collection much more valuable. Undoubtedly the additional series of art cards would contain cowboy subjects as well as possibly more cowgirls. This is a linen card. *From the private collection of Jack Davis, Olde America Antiques*

Judging from the costume this cowgirl wears, this might be a post WWII art card which promotes the friendly west. Note the squirrel on her knee. On the reverse is the following: "Natural color post card made in U.S.A. by E.C. Kropp Co., Milwaukee, Wis." *Author's Collection*

Cowgirls were very popular for advertising various products. In this art card, a cowgirl holds a Sharps promoting the C.C. Knight Company, merchants in structural materials. On the reverse is the slogan "You will find our representative on the other side out gunning for orders..." *From the private collection of Jack Davis, Olde America Antiques*

Promoting the Stetson hat is the lovely art card sent by Hirshfelds & Anderson of Austin, Texas to their clients. *Author's Collection*

Dated 1909, this photo art card was taken by D. B. McFarland of Presho, South Dakota. He has titled this one "Queen of the West Rough Rider." *Author's Collection*

Cow Girl, Western Nebraska.

A photo art card image was often used with different captions. Here it is entitled "Cow Girl, Western Nebraska," yet the same image has been published using the title "A Wyoming Cow Girl." These photo art cards romancing the cowgirl, were issued in 1910 by Miller Brothers Publishing of Alliance, Nebraska. *Author's Collection*

"IT'S A WAY THEY HAVE IN IDAHO"

A healthy looking, confident cowgirl challenges the viewer with her hand on her pistol. Entitled "It's a way they have in Idaho," it is a photo art card published by Faust's Art Store in Boise, Idaho. This black and white card was actually printed in Germany. *Author's Collection*

The popularity of the American western cowboy and cowgirl is exemplified in this black and white photo art card published in Europe for that market. Note the title on the card "Burgos and Clara Western Amerikan Novelty." *From the private collection of Jack Davis, Olde America Antiques*

Burgos and Clara
Western Amerikan Novelty

The round up

Romancing the cowgirl by the cowboy is a common theme seen here in this sensitive portrayal of "The round up," a photo art card. Often used for communications between lovers, these cards were extremely popular from 1906 through 1915. *Author's Collection*

In a copyright 1907 photo art card by W.G. MacFarlane is another image of a cowboy wooing a cowgirl again with the title "The Round-up." Note the cowgirl is removing the cowboy's pistol from his holster, behind his back! *Author's Collection*

Cowboy Series—"The Round-up."
Copyright 1907 by W. G. MacFarlane

A colorful postcard advertising a strong fence. Note standing assertive cowgirl. *From the Thomas B. Martin Memorial Museum, Inc.*

DON'T STOP THE GAME, PAGE FENCE WILL STOP THEM.

Calvert Lith. Co., Detroit

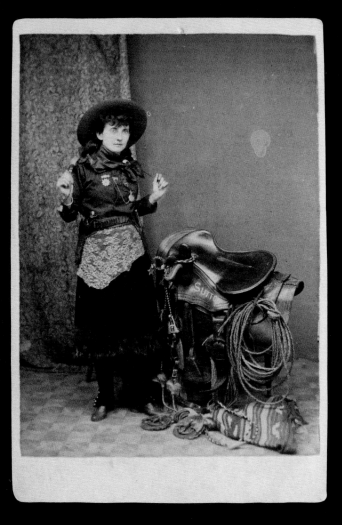

A rare pose on this cabinet photo shows Prairie Pearl, Mrs. H.J. Sutton, posing with her personalized side-saddle. *From the Thomas B. Martin Memorial Museum, Inc.*

Two performers, possibly husband and wife pose for a Rhode Island photographer in this rare cabinet-sized photo. Their outfits are complete with horse gear and firearms; a Colt Single Action in his holster and in the saddle holster. *From the Thomas B. Martin Memorial Museum, Inc.*

CHAPTER 5
COWGIRL THREE DIMENSIONAL COLLECTIBLES

Concentrating on clothing, hats, vests, scarves and gloves of the rodeo cowgirl, not to mention the horse-related accouterments, presents the collector with a very narrow selection. Oftentimes, there is little difference between what was 'cowgirl' and 'cowboy' which makes assembling a strictly cowgirl collection most difficult.

Split riding skirts which were obviously strictly for the women, were fabricated out of leather, some manufacturers actually used horsehide, while others used corduroy or other heavy material yet they wore out and were replaced regularly depending on the income of the cowgirl. For the most part, in the early years, the girls had to rely on their seamstress abilities to create some of their own fashions as commercially made clothing for the cowgirl was expensive and hard to find. If one girl was more adept at sewing and designing rodeo togs, she would often sew for other cowgirls and cowboys.

Colorful silk or satin shirts appealed to both sexes as did the vibrantly hued scarves and fancy boots. Hats were similar for both with only size being different; women's heads were apparently smaller! Women did fancy the beaded or embroidered vests and gloves also known as gauntlets. The beadwork for these special garments was generally done by the Indian women who often participated in the various rodeo events including the parades, grand entries and the "squaw" races.

However, when one considers the collection of any garments from any period, it is quickly understood that for the most part, clothing was utilized until it simply wore out. It was then discarded and replaced. Thus, finding apparel and the various accouterments of this era is an accomplishment requiring a sizable investment of time and money.

Split riding skirts, the ultimate cowgirl dimensional collectible, enjoy a wide range in value depending on condition, material used such as leather or corduroy and style. Should a skirt bear a label from a known maker such as Hamley's of Oregon for example, that would add considerably to its worth. Blouses are somewhat rare yet their value is again determined by maker label, and condition as are the various hats. Scarves which are unmarked are collectible, however the Pendleton Oregon Rodeo scarf which has an image, a colorful border and the phrase "Let 'er Buck" have a greater value in the eyes of the collector.

This phrase became so popular with the rodeo crowd, it could be found on other scarves or rodeo mufflers as they were called.

Saddles and bridles which are specifically designated "cowgirl" are those which currently reside in museum collections such as the Cowgirl Hall of Fame and the Cowboy Hall of Fame. These particular saddles ordinarily have been donated either by the cowgirl herself or by her family and can be identified with that specific performer. Frequently it is either a trick rider's saddle or prize piece won in a contest.

Naturally, if a particular collectible can be attributed to a specific cowgirl especially a 'name' cowgirl, that item becomes unparalleled in terms of value. The Gene Autry Heritage Center has a number of identifiable cowgirl items including Mabel Baker's spurs and various items from trick rider Bonnie Gray. The author has in her collection the riding togs and suitcase of Bertha Blancett, one of the earliest cowgirls known. Its value is priceless.

Gathering a representative collection featuring the cowgirl would not be complete without these three dimensional items. Their rarity should be recognized and their inherent values should be immensely protected for the cowgirl and the cowboy as well, are unique to America. Collectors of this fascinating genre perpetuate and preserve the American West.

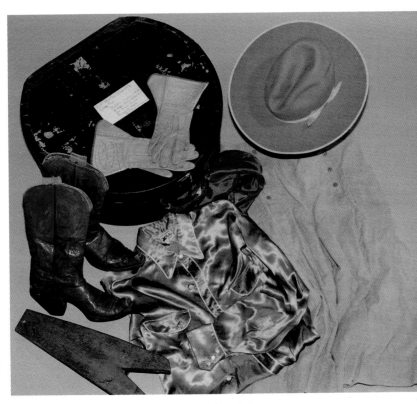

Collection of items from Bertha Blancett, early day rodeo cowgirl shows her corduroy split riding skirt, apple green satin rodeo blouse, purple neckerchief and leather gloves. Also included in this special collection is her hat, kidskin gloves, boots and a bootjack. Everything seen here can be stored in Bertha's round suitcase also shown. *Author's Collection*

An extremely rare pair of rodeo spurs from cowgirl Mabel Baker as photographed on a red rodeo shirt. Note the relief letters forming the name "Mabel." *Courtesy the Gene Autry Western Heritage Museum, Los Angeles*

This is a very rare selection of identifiable cowgirl items from well known trick rider Bonnie Gray. Her hat and trick riding boots are shown along with her favorite competitor number '13'. One of her trophies, a very rare item is included in this collection. *Courtesy the Gene Autry Western Heritage Museum, Los Angeles*

This is a very unusual selection of collectibles from an unknown cowgirl. In the picture of the cowgirl, she wears the actual bronco belt and leather cuffs shown here. The cuffs appear to be rather large and they are; however, note closely that the snap on the cuffs has been altered to fit a smaller wrist. A set of initials has also been secured onto the bronco belt. *Author's Collection*

Circa 1911 commercially made split riding skirt made by Wm. H. Hoegee Co. of Los Angeles, California is made of heavy cotton corduroy, unlined but reinforced at each inner leg. Serving as a bottom hem, the skirt has 7 rows of stitching. This is a very rare example of the split skirt designed with a flap which can be buttoned to one side giving it the appearance of a full street skirt. Traditionally this type of skirt was very long due to the fashion of the day. An interesting side note regarding this particular skirt is, through a series of events, it served as the prototype for many of the current replica maker's split skirts. This original served for many years as a movie costume piece.

A small bolero type vest is also shown along with lovely 1925 period ladies gauntlets. *Phil and Linda Spangenberger collection. Photo by Charlie Rathbun*

Label from the original riding skirt shown in the previous image, made by Wm. H. Hoegee Co. of Los Angeles. This skirt is listed as photo #7 in their 1911 catalog. *Phil and Linda Spangenberger collection. Photo by Charlie Rathbun*

A rare pair of August Bermann spurs used by a cowgirl as determined by their small size. Cast in bronze, this pair also has rather large spur straps and silver conchos indicating perhaps an earlier usage than 1900. *Author's Collection*

Produced by Hamley Co. of Pendleton, Oregon, this horsehide split riding skirt is complete with bottom fringe and full flap front snap closure. Note the adjustable buckles on the sides of the waistband. *Author's collection*

Inside the waistband, on the front of the skirt shown in the previous image is this label identifying it as produced by Hamley and Co. Cowboy Outfitters, Pendleton, Oregon. *Author's Collection*

Another Hamley split riding skirt, this one made of split cowhide has double rows of fringe on the bottom, yet is a similar style as the aforementioned skirt with full flap front snap closure and adjustable side waistband buckles. *Author's Collection*

Label from the waistband of the split cowhide Hamley skirt again shows the manufacturer Hamley & Co., Cowboy Outfitters, Pendleton, Oregon. *Author's Collection*

Another rare riding skirt, this made of split cowhide. From the collection of John Kopec, it is attributed to Johnsie Eager Thorn, wife of Joel Thorn who was a close friend and racing car partner of Howard Hughes. *From the John and Ruth Kopec collection*

Detail from Thorn skirt shows the buttons with a maker's name, N. Porter of Phoenix. *From the John and Ruth Kopec collection*

Catalog No. 12 from the N. Porter Saddle and Harness Co. of Phoenix, Arizona where the skirt is listed on page 65. *From the John and Ruth Kopec collection*

Catalog No. 12

N. PORTER SADDLE AND HARNESS CO. — Phoenix, Arizona

Riding Skirts

No. 32 Riding Skirt—Made out of golden brown glove leather, pliable and durable, with fringe as shown. Price $20.00

No. 33 Riding Skirt—Made out of finest quality smoked horsehide. This material will not scuff and will give many years of service. Price with fringe as shown..$32.50

No. 34 Same as No. 33, only plain without fringe. Price......................$30.00

No. 32—Riding Skirt

No. 27 Skirt—Made of soft brown glove leather, pliable and durable.
Price as shown......................$18.00
Price with fringe......................$20.00

No. 28 Skirt—Made same as No. 27, out of smoked horsehide.
Price without fringe......................$30.00
Price with fringe......................32.50

In ordering skirts give following measurements:
1. Measurement around waist.
2. Around hips in largest place.
3. Length from top of waist band to bottom of skirt.
4. Crotch measure. Measure from top of waist band in front, between legs and up to top of waist band in back.

No. 27—Skirt

We Pay the Postage — Page 65

N. PORTER SADDLE AND HARNESS CO. PHOENIX ARIZONA

A typical suede leather vest trimmed in smooth leather probably made for a cowgirl due to its small size, and closure placement. Note the studded trim around the scalloped leather edges and pockets. Vest is shown over a satin rodeo shirt. *Author's Collection*

The reverse side of the vest shows the continuation of the studded scalloped trim around the neck and bottom edge. In the center of the back is a fully beaded yellow flower. *Author's Collection*

Label from the cowgirl leather vest shows the manufacturer, The Cowboy Toggery located in Dubois, Wyoming. *Author's Collection*

A close up of the rodeo shirt label shows the maker as Ben the Rodeo Tailor located in Philadelphia, Pennsylvania. His slogan was "Maker of the finest in rodeo attire." *Author's Collection*

Clearly this is a satin shirt made for a cowboy, yet many cowgirls did wear their boyfriend's shirts. It is included here due to its beauty and unusual maker's location for a western rodeo shirt - Philadelphia, PA. Note the pearl snaps on the pockets and the sleeves. *Author's Collection*

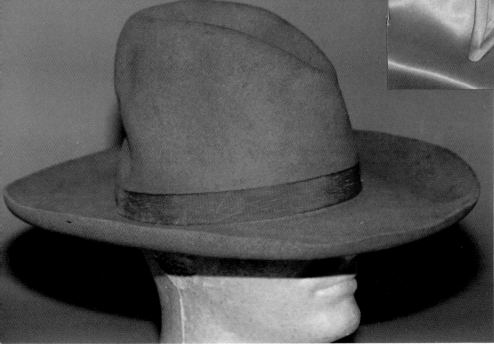

A very small sized felt type hat which was probably worn by a cowgirl but cannot be confirmed. It is from the Helbing Hat Company and bears a gold stamp on the inside hat brim "Number 1 Special Quality." *Author's Collection*

One of several pairs of beaded gauntlets included in this collection, this brain-tanned buckskin pair has been beaded with forest green, pink and blue tiny seed beads. Many gauntlets were fringed, adding to their flashiness. *Author's Collection*

A lovely pair of smoke tanned hide gauntlets, often called "Crow Cuffs," were made around the mid 1920s to early 1930s. They are small sized, fringed and appear to be Indian made, with the cuffs lined in colored calico cloth. *Phil & Linda Spangenberger collection. Photo by Charlie Rathbun*

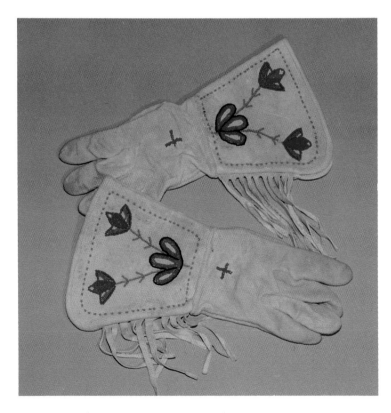

Beaded gauntlets are rare but can be found. The smaller sized pairs are especially difficult to locate. Here is a lovely brain tanned buckskin, beaded and fringed pair, probably for a cowgirl based on the size. *Author's Collection*

A pair of white brain tanned buckskin, Indian made gauntlets, circa 1910-1930 which have calico cotton lined cuffs and a lovely pinked edge along the upper cuff border. Fringed, they are very small in size. *Phil & Linda Spangenberger collection. Photo by Charlie Rathbun*

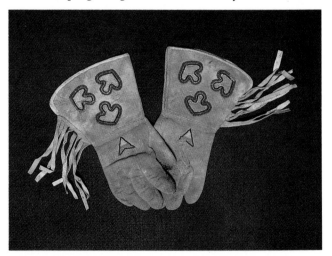

Circa 1920-1930s woman's sized, Indian made gauntlets, white brained tanned buckskin, again with the inside cuff lined in colored calico cloth. This is unique pair as the cuff portion is stiffened to maintain a true 'cuff' effect. *Phil & Linda Spangenberger collection. Photo by Charlie Rathbun*

An unusual pair of heavily fringed, commercially made gauntlets from the Frank Russell Glove Company out of Berlin, Wisconsin. They feature an expanding gusset in the stitched cuff of each glove and probably date from the 1920s or 1930s. The cuff edges are cloth bound. *Phil & Linda Spangenberger collection. Photo by Charlie Rathbun*

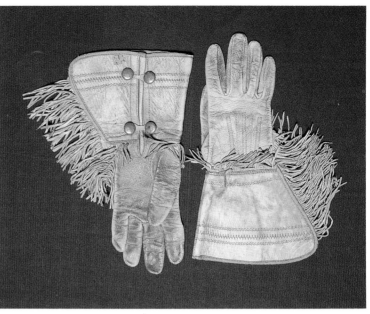

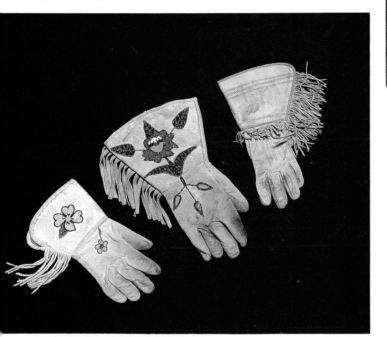

One way to tell if a pair of gauntlets was made for a woman is to compare the size with an obvious man's glove. Note the gauntlet in the center is an Indian made example, circa 1900-1920 of smoke tanned buckskin and is about size 8 1/2 making it a medium man's hand size. The Indian made brain tanned white buckskin glove at left is much smaller and therefore better suited to a slender woman's hand as is the commercially manufactured gray/tan buckskin gauntlet at the right. The commercial product is much finer fitting than is the more primitive hand cut Indian piece, yet it is too slender a fit for a man's broader hand.

Phil & Linda Spangenberger collection. Photo by Charlie Rathbun

A beautifully beaded floral pair of ladies fringed gauntlets from the 1930s made of Indian brain tanned buckskin. Note the different colors of beads used and the similarity of the beadwork patterns. *Author's Collection*

An interesting smoke tanned, moose hide pair of embroidered gauntlets, probably worn by a rodeo performer after the turn of the century. Indians often used color thread and embroidered designs when beads were unavailable, generally during the reservation period. *Author's collection*

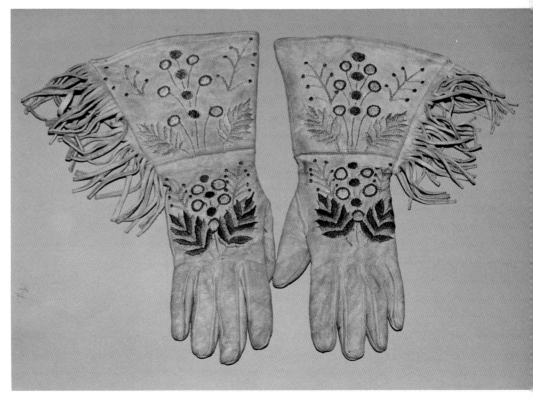

A beautiful pair of leather gauntlets with no embroidery or beadwork but rather an embossed design of a cowgirl. An unusual pair complete with fringe. *From the Thomas B. Martin Memorial Museum, Inc.*

Detail from gauntlets shows embossed cowgirl design. Is she yearning for the wide open plains of the west? *From the Thomas B. Martin Memorial Museum, Inc.*

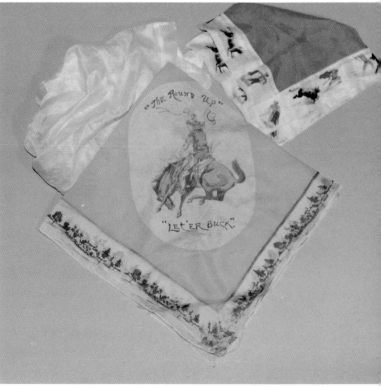

Scarves or rodeo mufflers were used by the early cowboys as a utilitarian item for keeping the dust out of their noses, washing, etc. As the rodeo sport became more popular, the scarf became a decorative item, especially for the cowgirls and the rodeo fans. Shown is one of the more rare items, a bordered scarf from the Pendleton Round Up with the famous logo and title "Let 'er Buck." Also shown is a rare colorful scarf showing a bullfight image along the border. In the background is a lovely white scarf favored by the ladies in their studio photos. *Author's Collection*

No. 307-FI   14½ to 18. Postage paid $1.00   No. 310-FI

RODEO MUFFLERS

No. 311-FI

No. 312-FI

No. 313-FI

No. 311-FI—Cowboy Silk Mufflers of extra heavy pure silk. This muffler is extra quality thru and thru and will give more than usual service. Rider design in corner, plain colored border. Colors are Red, Green, Purple, Cerise, Blue or Orange. Large size, 30 inches square. Postage paid **75c**

No. 312-FI—"The Round-Up" Silk Muffler—Tied and Dyed design—a light weight, dressy muffler in 27-inch size. Colors are Green, Red, Purple, Blue or Orange. Protect yourself from heat and winds.
—WEAR A MUFFLER. **45c**
Postage paid ....

No. 313-FI—Solid color Rodeo Muffler Star and Flower embroidered design in ner. The excellent silk, fine finish and l size (30 inches square) makes this mu one of the best to be had. Colors are Green, Yellow, Purple, Cerise, or Black. Postage paid **75**

Solid color Silk Mufflers, hemstitched bor Dressy, light weight and colorful. Typl Western in color and style. Plain Black, Green, Yellow or Purple. In two sizes:
No. 314-FI—27 inches square
Postage paid **35**
No. 315-FI—29 inches square
Postage paid **45**

A Catalogue of Western Supplies
FOR SPRING AND SUMMER 1936
NUMBER FORTY-FIVE

White and Davis
PUEBLO, COLORADO
The West's Own Store Since 1889 :: 47 Years Of "Always Reliable" Service

From a period catalog offering rodeo mufflers either with or without the well-known saying "Let 'er Buck." *Author's collection*

Here is the cover of the catalog which has the rodeo mufflers. These catalogs make excellent reference resources.

With the popularity of the cowgirl, rodeos and the like, the little ladies in the 1950s dreamed of wearing their own rodeo togs. Shown here is a split cowhide outfit including a riding skirt and vest trimmed in red suede. It is approximately a child's size 3. *Author's Collection*

Identifying whether a pair of boots was worn by a cowgirl or cowboy is difficult, yet some determination is possible based on size. While the boots pictured here are not very fancy, it is known that they were used by a cowgirl. With the tops of the boots measuring a short 12" they were used probably in the 1940s. *Author's Collection*

Souvenirs from the various rodeos are very rare and collectible. Shown is a Pendleton pennant from the 1950s along with a small leather Pendleton, Oregon photo album dated 1930. Photos inside show a family's trip 'out west' to see the fabled Pendleton Oregon Round Up. *Author's Collection*

Pins, stickers and the like were also souvenirs from the various Wild West shows and rodeos. Shown on the left, a pin type button from a 1930s rodeo states "Ride 'em Cowboy." On the right is a sticker measuring about 3 1/2" across, from the Cheyenne Frontier Days. Judging from the artwork it could be dated as from the 1930s. Due to their fragility, many of these stickers probably did not survive the years, making them very rare items. *Author's Collection*

This image has been used on art postcards and is shown here on the cover of a very popular early 1900s sheet music called *"Cheyenne."* A series of 4 photo postcards based on the lyrics of this song was shown in an earlier chapter of this book. A very popular courting song. *Author's Collection*

Lovely cowgirls were often used for the covers of sheet music, a very popular item. Here is a cutie on the cover of original sheet music for THE FLOWER OF THE RANCH by Joseph Howard. *Author's Collection*

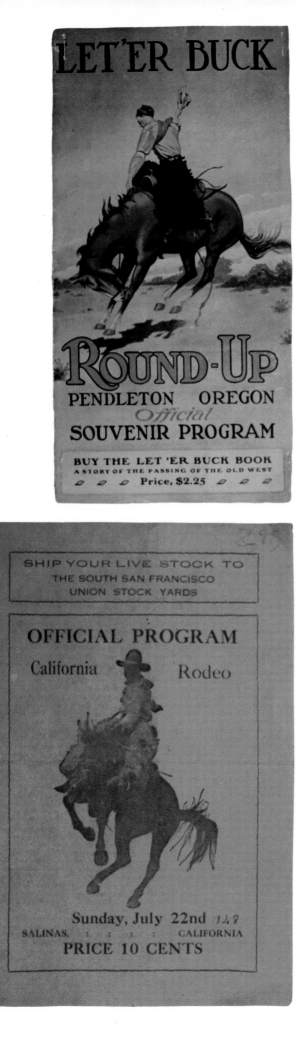

Original rodeo programs have become very collectible not only for their wealth of information but for the lovely artwork and printing. Shown here is a full color fold out type rodeo program from the Pendleton Oregon Round Up. This color, single page, folded program was printed with contestants for individual days listed inside. This one is listed as the Official Souvenir Round Up Program for Thursday, September 22nd. (No year printed). It measures 12 1/4" tall by 5 1/2" wide.

Because a full color advertisement for the Pendleton Woolen Mills appears on the inside, it could be concluded that they were the sponsor for the printing of the program. Inside the program is the following statement:

"The only, original Round Up. The epic drama of the west. Owned by the City of Pendleton, staged by volunteer organizations, pays neither salaries nor dividends. A panorama of the Old West, the Frontier, Plains, Mountains and Ranges. Wild and wooly, fast and bully. Originators of Let'er Buck. Mail this souvenir program to your friends - postage one cent." *Author's Collection*

A program from the Second Annual Roundup from Bozeman, Montana held August 5,6,7 in 1920. Inside are articles on rodeo events, advertisements for elections of the various political figures of the day and promotional information about the area. Inserted into the program is the listing of participating performers and contestants which changed daily. Overall it measures 8 1/2" tall by 5 1/2" wide. *Author's Collection*

Perhaps not as flamboyant as the Pendleton Round-Up is this simple two page program from the 1928 Salinas, California Rodeo. This program measures 11" tall by 7" wide. *Author's Collection*

From the biggest rodeo event of that year, a full color program of the 1926 Tex Austin Chicago Rodeo. Here many of the World Champions were determined. A very rare, collectible item providing much needed information on the cowgirls as well as cowboys. Note the line at the bottom of the program..."This program not complete with daily program insert." Dimensions; 11 1/4" tall by 8 1/4" wide. *Author's Collection*

"*In Oklahoma*" is the title of this original sheet music which features a lovely artistic rendition of what a cowgirl wore on the plains. A beautiful item. *Author's Collection*

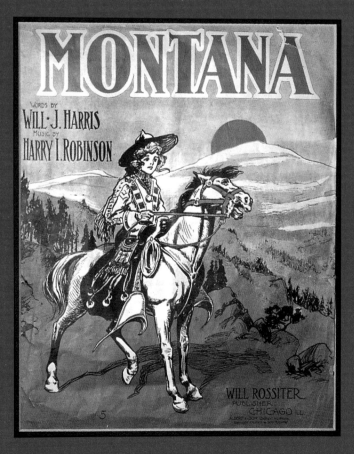

Sheet music dating from 1905 where a beautifully clad cowgirl is dressed complete with her Indian buckskins, split riding skirt and beaded pipe bag tucked at her waist. It is simply called *"Montana."* *Phil & Linda Spangenberger collection. Photo by Charlie Rathbun.*

Due to their popularity, cowgirls were used on everything to promote various products. Shown here is a cowgirl on the label of "Golden West Coffee" produced by Closset and Devers out of Portland, Oregon. This glass jar with red screw top measures 6 1/2" tall. *Author's Collection*

In an antique frame dating from the 1910s is this lovely image of a cowgirl wearing her hair in long braids and with a low-slung, flap holster and belt set around her waist. It measures 16" X 13." *Author's Collection*

An unusual 1890s color lithograph by Hayes Litho of Buffalo, New York shows a fantasy based cowgirl roping a steer, from the off side. Measuring 8" X 12" it was also available in postcard form. *Author's Collection*

Another cowgirl image on this later calendar dated 1926 from "John Krabania, The Fashion, Kingman, Ariz." It is rare to find early calendars in fine condition complete with the entire set of months attached. *From the private collection of Jack Davis, Olde America Antiques*

Typical of the day, this romantic image of a cowgirl graces an early, 1918 calendar which was complimentary from "E.D. Kratzer, Restaurant and Confectionery." The overall size is 11" tall by 7" wide. *Author's Collection*

A highly romantic image of a model posing as a cowgirl complete with a gun on her hip. Taken from an early day calendar it measures 12 1/2" X 9" excluding modern frame. *Author's Collection*

Included in this series of three dimensional collectibles is the reverse side of an early 1912 postcard from Pendleton, Oregon. Oftentimes collectors ignore the reverse side of these collectibles focusing on the image printed on the front. This is interesting not only for the 1912 post office cancellation, it is a request for a fall catalog of Meier and Frank in Pendleton, a popular leather goods manufacturer of the period. *Author's Collection*

It is difficult to identify whether horse gear was used by a cowgirl or cowboy. This is included in this collection because of the unusually large cheek pieces seen fully studded on this headstall, favored by the cowgirls. Note the crude hand-forged bit. *Author's Collection*

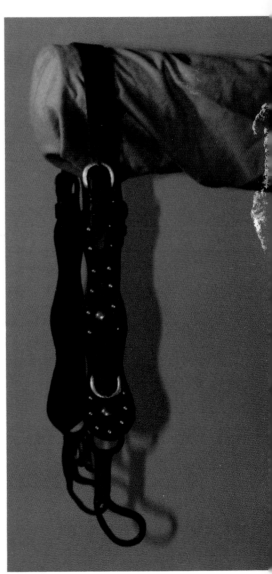

This is an unusual set featuring a business card holder including business cards from Newman Bartlett who was an advance agent for the 101 Ranch Wild West Show. Unique, as it has two other business cards for the same individual, one of which is as representative for the Boston Ideal Comic Opera. No doubt, this man was an agent for performing rodeo contestants. *Author's Collection*

A beautiful headstall made of hand-tooled leather, silver conchos and a reproduction of an early type Garcia Bit. Flashy piece of horse gear possibly used by a cowgirl. *Author's Collection*

A typical saddle which could have been used by a cowgirl, made by Meanea of Cheyenne, Wyoming. *Author's Collection*

Close up of previous horse headstall showing the leather detail. *Author's Collection*

Detail of saddle skirt shown in previous image showing the maker's stamp of F.A. Meanea, Maker, Cheyenne, Wyo. *Author's Collection*

Thankfully there were several items donated to museums so that the interested public may view these magnificent artifacts left by these colorful ladies. Here is a trophy saddle made by Hamley and Co. from Pendleton, Oregon, once owned by recognized cowgirl Lorena Trickey. *Courtesy National Cowboy Hall of Fame and Western Heritage Center*

Also housed in a museum is the trick saddle used by fabled cowgirl Tad Lucas. This beauty was made by Atkins Ryon of Fort Worth, Texas. *Courtesy National Cowboy Hall of Fame and Western Heritage Center*

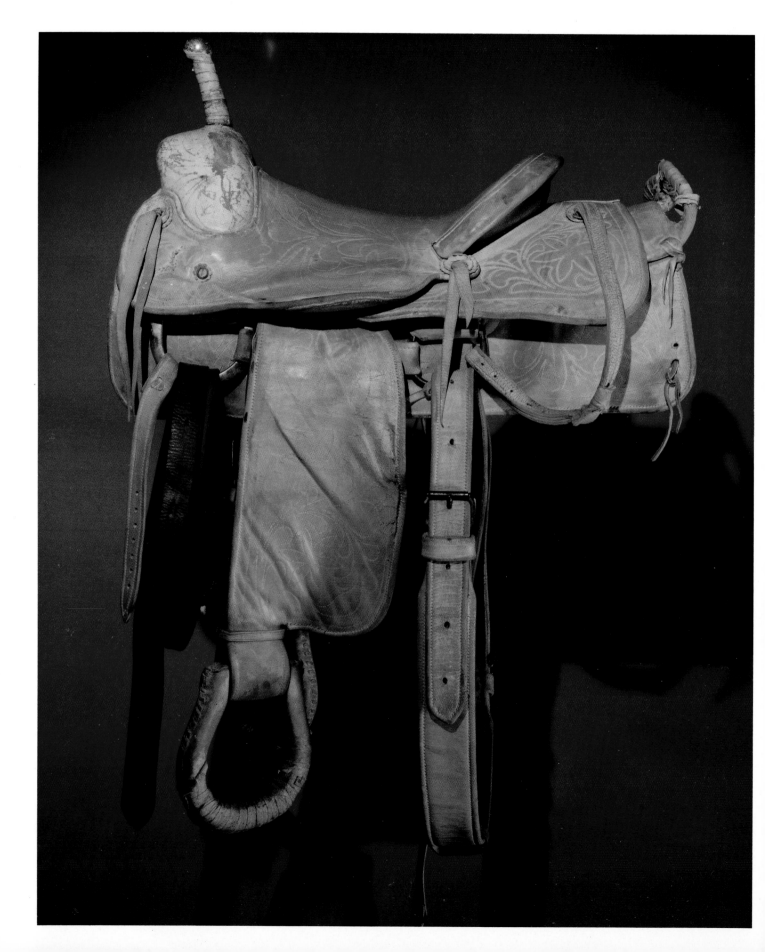

BIBLIOGRAPHY

BOOKS

Freeman, *Danny. World's Oldest Rodeo.* Prescott Frontier Days, Inc. 1988.

Furlong, Charles Wellington. *Let'er Buck.* New York: G. P. Putnam's Sons The Knickerbocker Press, 1921.

Jordan, Teresa. *Cowgirls, Women of the American West.* Anchor Press/Doubleday, 1982.

McGinnis, Vera. *Rodeo Road.* Hastings House, 1974

Porter, Willard H. *Who's Who In Rodeo.* Oklahoma City: Powder River Book Company, 1982.

Riske, Milt, *Those Magnificent Cowgirls: A History of the Rodeo Cowgirl.* Wyoming Publishing, 1983.

Roach, Joyce Gibson. *The Cowgirls.* Cordovan Corporation, 1977.

Sayers, Isabelle S. *Annie Oakley and Buffalo Bill's Wild West.* Dover Publications, Inc. 1981.

Sloan, Dorothy. *Women In the Cattle Country; Catalogue Three.* Private printing, 1986.

Stansbury, Kathryn B. *Lucille Mulhall, Her Family, Her Life, Her Times.* Private Printing, 1985.

Wood-Clark, Sarah. *Beautiful Daring Western Girls: Women of the Wild West.* Catalogue prepared for an exhibition at the Buffalo Bill Historical Center, Wyoming, 1985.

ARTICLES

Bird, Roy and Luann. " 'Punkin Roller' Rodeos A Little Touch of the Old West." *Journal of the West,* Vol. XVII, No. 3, (July 1978).

Blake, Tona and Stiffler, Liz. "Fannie Sperry-Steele Montana's Champion Bronc Rider." *Montana: the Magazine of Western History,* Spring 1982.

Cohen, Cassy Mahoney. "Turk Greenough." *Persimmon Hill,* Vol. 10, No.2, 1980.

Coster, Eric. "Salinas Rodeo." *Persimmon Hill,* Vol. 6, No.3, 1976.

Gray, Sally. "Tad Lucas...her world of Rodeo." *Persimmon Hill.* Vol. 9, No.4, 1980.

Greenough, Alice. "Cowgirls of Yesterday." *Persimmon Hill,* Vol. 4, No.3, 1974.

Jordan, Teresa. "Alice Greenough." *Persimmon Hill,* Vol. 12, No.1, 1982.

Palen, J.S. "Cheyenne Frontier Days." *Persimmon Hill,* Vol. 7, No.3, 1977.

Porter, Willard H. "They Clicked in Rodeo." *Persimmon Hill,* Vol. 6, No.4, 1976.

Porter, Willard H. "When They Took The West to London." *True West,* September 1985.

Remley, Mary L. "From Sidesaddle to Rodeo." *Journal of the Old West,* Vol. XVII, No. 3. (July 1978).

Singleton, Carrie "The Powder Puff Buckaroos." *Northwest Magazine,* July 1976.

Williams, George. "C.B. Irwin High Roller." *Persimmon Hill,* Vol. 7 No.2, 1977.

Williams, George. "A Real Hand Dick Shelton." *Persimmon Hill,* Vol. 6, No.1, 1976.

MISCELLANEOUS

Blancett, Bertha; Correspondence with relatives, original letters in author collection.

Burson, Polly; oral historical interview with author 1993.

Engel Auction Catalogs

Hammer, MaryLou; oral historical interview with author 1989, 1990, 1993.

High Noon Auction Catalogs

Lucas, Tad; correspondence with author 1984, 1986.

National Cowgirl Hall of Fame archives.

Original 101 Ranch program dated 1910 in author's collection.

Original Rodeo Programs: Pendleton Round-Up 1925; Pendleton Round-Up year not indicated; Salinas California 1928; Second Annual Round Up Bozeman Montana 1920; Chicago Rodeo 1926 all in author's collection.

The Wild Bunch Newsletter from the Rodeo Hall of Fame, Vol. 1, No.1, July, 1975.

INDEX

PRICE GUIDE

As most serious collectors realize, placing values on items such as those in this book is an extremely difficult task. Yet, prices listed have been estimated based on recent auctions, collector's shows, items available from dealers as well as from other collectors. When searching a value, bear in mind the condition of the piece, the area of the country where it is located and the true rarity of the collectible. The values listed below are intended for use as a guide only, and are not in any way designed to serve as a definitive price control. With the growing popularity of the western collectibles spreading rapidly throughout the world, the natural result of supply and demand will continue to escalate prices.

Chapter 1, photo postcards of identified individuals and/or rodeos range in value from $100 - $175. Unidentified, $25 - $75.

Chapter 2, group photo postcards; identified $175 - $225; unidentified, $75 - $100.

Chapter 3, rodeo scene photo postcards; identified $100 - $125; unidentified $35 - $75.

Chapter 4, photo art cards $35 - $50; art cards $45 - $65 yet can go higher depending on fame of artist.

PAGE NUMBER	POSITION CODE	VALUE
1	PHOTO	$75 - $100
2	PHOTO	$1750-$2500
52	BL 11" x 14" SIZE	$225
72	L	$100
72	R	$135
73	L	$135
73	R	$135
74	L	$150
74	R	$150
75	L	$150
75	R	$150
76	L	$135
76	R	$175
77	L	$200
77	R	$200
78	L	$225
78	R	$375
79	TL	$35
79	BL	$35
79	CR	$35
80	T	$150
80	B	$175
81	T	$125
81	CL	$125
81	BR	$150
82	L	$150

PAGE NUMBER	POSITION CODE	VALUE
82	R	$150
83	TL	$150
83	TR	$150
83	BL	$150
83	BR	$150
100	TL	$325
100	BR	$425
101	BR	$5500
102	TL	$1375
102	CR	$5000
102	BC	$1750
103	TL-SKIRT	$950 - $1750
103	TL-VEST	$450
103	TL-GAUNTLETS	$475
103	BR	$425
104	TL	$950 - $1750
104	BR	$950 - $1750
105	TL	$950 - $1750
105	BL	$225
106	VEST	$575
107	TL	$325
107	BL	$225
108	GAUNTLETS	$375 - $625
109	GAUNTLETS	$375 - $625
110	T	$325
110	CL	$150
110	BR	$150
111	TR	$175
111	CL	$175
111	BR	$325
112	PENNANT	$75
112	ALBUM	$50
112	BUTTON	$75
112	STICKER	$75
112	BL	$50
112	BR	$50
113	TL	$35
113	CR	$25
113	BL	$25
114	TL	$45
114	CR	$50
114	BL	$50
115	TL	$125
115	CR	$135
115	BL	$225
116	TL	$150
116	CR	$150
116	BL	$125
117	TL	$150
117	BR	$375
117	BL	$225
118	TL	$375
118	TR	$2500

The abbreviations for the position code are as follows: L = left, R = right, TL = top left, TR = top right, CR = center right, CL = center left, BR = bottom right, BL = bottom left

Back Cover Photos

Back Left
Decidedly a romantic, luscious interpretation of the American cowgirl by impressionist artist S. Peterson is printed in full color on this 1910 art card. Entitled "The Echoing Call of the Cowgirl" it is part of the "Cow Boy Series" published by H.H. Tammen, Denver, Colorado. *Author's Collection*

Back Top Right
Another Peterson full color art card copyrighted in 1909 by H.H. Tammen depicts two "Western Thoroughbreds," the cowgirl and her horse. *Author's Collection*

Back Top Left
Peterson again captures the romance of the cowgirl in this roping image on a full color art card. *From the private collection of Jack Davis, Olde America Antiques*